Gretchen Bitterlin
Dennis Johnson
Donna Price
Sylvia Ramirez
K. Lynn Savage, Series Editor

Ventures 1

WORKBOOK

CAMBRIDGE
UNIVERSITY PRESS

Contents

Get ready

1 Write the words.

area	first	last	middle	telephone	zip

1. ___*first*___

2. _____ → name

3. _____

4. _____ → number

5. _____ → code

6. _____

2 Write the words.

area code	last name	telephone number
first name	middle name	zip code

1. (Linda) May Parker _____*first name*_____

2. (718)-555-1234 _____

3. Linda May (Parker) _____

4. 718-(555-1234) _____

5. Linda (May) Parker _____

6. New York, NY (10012) _____

Check your answers. See page 127.

Personal information

3 Match the questions with the answers.

1. What is your name? _b_   a. 10012
2. What is your first name? ____   b. Yuki Yamamoto
3. What is your last name? ____   c. 555-1234
4. What is your zip code? ____   d. Yamamoto
5. What is your telephone number? ____   e. Yuki

4 Write the words.

address	area code	first name	last name	telephone number

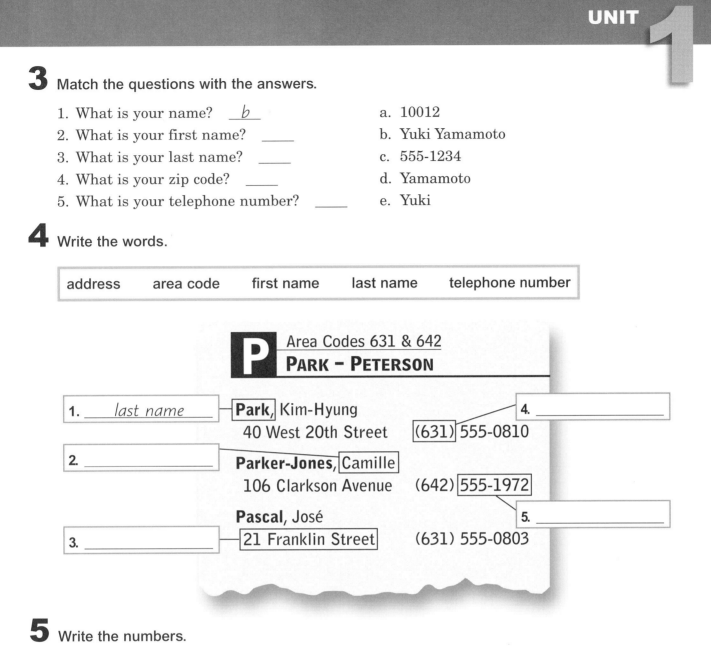

P Area Codes 631 & 642
PARK - PETERSON

1. ___last name___ —┤**Park**, Kim-Hyung   4. _____
    40 West 20th Street (631) 555-0810

2. _____ **Parker-Jones**, Camille
    106 Clarkson Avenue (642) 555-1972

    Pascal, José   5. _____
3. _____ —┤21 Franklin Street (631) 555-0803

5 Write the numbers.

1. (six three one) five five five – seven eight one oh

   _(631) 555-7810_

2. (six four two) five five five – one nine seven two

   _____

3. (four three two) five five five – nine eight oh three

   _____

4. (seven nine eight) five five five – six four two one

   _____

Check your answers. See page 127.

What's your name?

Study the chart on page 123.

1 Match the questions with the answers.

1. What's his middle name? ___f___
2. What's her telephone number? ____
3. What's your last name? ____
4. What's their zip code? ____
5. What's her first name? ____
6. What's your area code? ____
7. What's his name? ____
8. What's their area code? ____

a. Their zip code is 85713.
b. Her first name is Jenna.
c. Her telephone number is 555-2758.
d. His name is Asad.
e. Their area code is 512.
f. His middle name is James.
g. My area code is 305.
h. My last name is Tran.

2 Complete the sentences. Use *her*, *his*, or *their*.

1. **A** What's ___his___ first name?

   B ___His___ first name is Hong-Zhi.

2. **A** What's _____ area code?

   B _____ area code is 808.

3. **A** What's _____ last name?

   B _____ last name is Kulik.

4. **A** What's _____ telephone number?

   B _____ telephone number is 555-1850.

3 Read the advertisement. Circle the answers.

1. What is Tina's last name?
   a. Jane
   (b.) Rodriguez

2. What is Tina's area code?
   a. 555
   b. 415

3. What is Tina's cell phone number?
   a. (415) 555-8221
   b. (415) 555-9214

Situations Wanted

Babysitter for Hire
Tina Jane Rodriguez: Experienced mother and child-care worker. San Francisco area.
Call Tina at
(415) 555-8221 (home) or
(415) 555-9214 (cell).

Check your answers. See page 127.

4 Complete the sentences. Use *her*, *his*, or *their*.

1. **A** What's ___his___ name?

   B _____ name is Coach Jones.

2. **A** What's _____ name?

   B _____ name is Mrs. Jones.

3. **A** What's _____ name?

   B _____ name is the Little Eagles.

5 Look at the pictures. Write sentences.

John Brown-Hudson

His name is John
Brown-Hudson.
(name)

Mary Wilson

_____
(first name)

Mr. and Mrs. Lopez

_____
(last name)

(608) 555-1234

_____
(area code)

02455

_____
(zip code)

555-1234

_____
(telephone number)

Check your answers. See page 127.

Study the chart on page 122.

1 Complete the sentences. Use contractions.

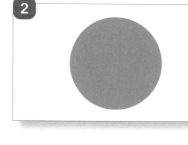

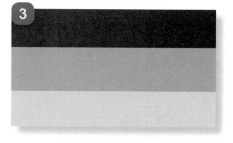

_We're_ from Canada.
(We are)

_____ from Japan.
(They are)

_____ from Germany.
(He is)

_____ from Somalia.
(She is)

_____ from Guatemala.
(I am)

_____ from Brazil.
(They are)

2 Write sentences.

1. from / She's / Ecuador / . _She's from Ecuador._

2. Chile / He's / from / . _____

3. He / from / Honduras / isn't / . _____

4. They're / Colombia / from / . _____

5. the Ukraine / You're / from / . _____

6. Pakistan / from / They're / . _____

7. They / Poland / from / aren't / . _____

8. She / isn't / Peru / from / . _____

9. You / from / aren't / Vietnam / . _____

10. El Salvador / She's / from / . _____

Check your answers. See page 127.

3 Look at the pictures. Answer the questions.

China

Korea

1. **A** Is he from Brazil?

   B ___No___ , ___he___ ___isn't___ .

2. **A** Is he from China?

   B _____ , _____ _____ .

3. **A** Is she from the United States?

   B _____ , _____ _____ .

4. **A** Is she from Korea?

   B _____ , _____ _____ .

Mexico

India

5. **A** Are you from Peru?

   B _____ , _____ _____ .

6. **A** Are you from Mexico?

   B _____ , _____ _____ .

7. **A** Are they from Somalia?

   B _____ , _____ _____ .

8. **A** Are they from India?

   B _____ , _____ _____ .

4 Complete the sentences. Use *am*, *are*, or *is*.

1. **A** What ___is___ your last name?

   B My last name _____ Sanchez.

2. **A** _____ you from the United States?

   B No, I _____ from Mexico.

3. **A** _____ she from the United States?

   B Yes, she _____ .

4. **A** Where _____ Mariya and Ivan from?

   B They _____ from Russia.

5. **A** What _____ their last name?

   B Their last name _____ Chernov.

6. **A** What _____ her telephone number?

   B Her telephone number _____ 555-9763.

Check your answers. See page 127.

1 Find the words.

address	city	signature	street	zip code
apartment	initial	state	title	

```
t  i  t  l  e  m  r  a  t  i
e  n  c  i  t  y  g  a  i  a
z  i  p  c  o  d  e  p  i  s
s  t  t  r  u  t  n  a  s  a
s  i  g  n  a  t  u  r  e  e
n  a  i  e  s  t  a  t  e  e
n  l  e  i  n  t  n  m  d  e
d  g  e  a  d  d  r  e  s  s
r  r  o  a  t  a  n  n  n  y
n  n  s  t  r  e  e  t  t  a
```

2 Write the words from Exercise 1 on the letter.

2. _____

1. _____title_____

Miss Sally R. Martinez

4. _____

497 Poplar Street, #3

3. _____

Madison, WI 53703

5. _____

Dear Mr. Li,

6. _____   7. _____   8. _____

~~may reach me at the address above with your response.~~

Thank you,

Sally Martinez

9. _____

Check your answers. See page 127.

3 Read the questions. Circle the answers.

1. What's his name?
   - (a.) His name is Juan.
   - b. My name is Juan.

2. What country is he from?
   - a. He's from Puerto Rico.
   - b. I'm from Puerto Rico.

3. What's his last name?
   - a. His last name is Cabrera.
   - b. Her last name is Carlos.

4. What is his area code?
   - a. His area code is 555-3461.
   - b. His area code is 813.

5. What is his zip code?
   - a. His zip code is 813.
   - b. His zip code is 33629.

6. What's his city?
   - a. His city is Clark Avenue.
   - b. His city is Tampa.

4 Read the story. Complete the ID card.

> Juan Cabrera is a new student. He's from Puerto Rico. His middle name is Carlos. His address is 138 Clark Avenue, Apt. 6, Tampa, Florida. His zip code is 33629. His telephone number is 555-3461. His area code is 813.

STUDENT ID

Name _Cabrera_ _____ _____
        Last   First   Middle

Address _____

        _____ _____ _____
           City   State   Zip code

Phone (_____) _____-_____

Check your answers. See page 127.

1 Write sentences.

1. China / are / They / from / .

   They are from China.

2. from / Where / you / are / ?

   _____

3. is / her / middle name / Mary / .

   _____

4. last name / her / is / What / ?

   _____

5. you / spell / How / do / that / ?

   _____

6. His / 1241 Washington Avenue / is / address / .

   _____

7. is / telephone number / What / your / ?

   _____

8. 202 / Their / is / area code / .

   _____

2 Correct the sentences. Add capital letters.

    H   B J

1. his name is bill jackson.

2. he is a new student.

3. his address is 371 purdy avenue.

4. his telephone number is 555-7819.

5. he is from new york.

Check your answers. See page 117.

3 Read the business card. Complete the sentences.

Premier Landscaping
Large or small, we do it all.

Robert R. Rodriguez
57 Bridge Road
Orange Park, FL 32073
(559) 555-7579

address	area code	last name	middle initial	telephone number	zip code

1. His ___last name___ is Rodriguez.

2. His _____ is 559.

3. His _____ is 32073.

4. His _____ is 555-7579.

5. His _____ is 57 Bridge Road.

6. His _____ is R.

4 Write a conversation. Use the sentences in the box.

Speaker A	Speaker B
My telephone number is (545) 555-7771.	Hi, Terri. What's your last name?
I'm Terri.	OK, what's your telephone number?
My last name is Smith.	Thanks. We'll call you soon.

1. **A** I'm Terri. _____

2. **B** _____
   _____

3. **A** _____
   _____

4. **B** _____
   _____

5. **A** _____
   _____

6. **B** _____
   _____

Check your answers. See page 128.

Another view

1 Look at the student identification card. Answer the questions.

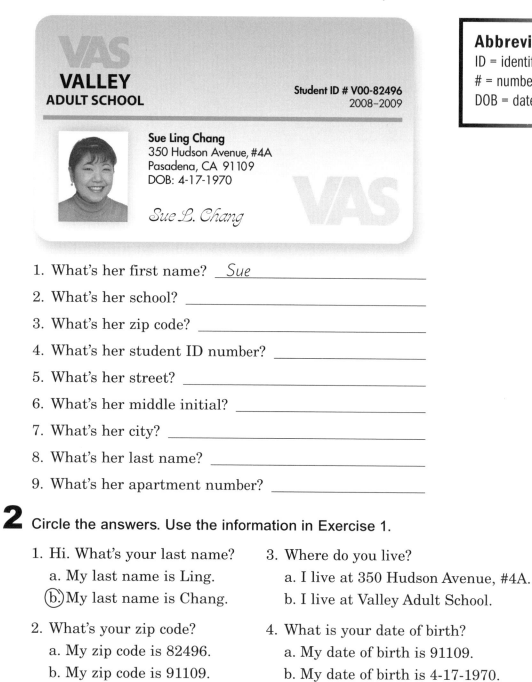

VALLEY
ADULT SCHOOL

Student ID # V00-82496
2008–2009

Sue Ling Chang
350 Hudson Avenue, #4A
Pasadena, CA 91109
DOB: 4-17-1970

Sue L. Chang

Abbreviations
ID = identification
# = number
DOB = date of birth

1. What's her first name? _Sue_____

2. What's her school? _____

3. What's her zip code? _____

4. What's her student ID number? _____

5. What's her street? _____

6. What's her middle initial? _____

7. What's her city? _____

8. What's her last name? _____

9. What's her apartment number? _____

2 Circle the answers. Use the information in Exercise 1.

1. Hi. What's your last name?
   a. My last name is Ling.
   b. My last name is Chang.

2. What's your zip code?
   a. My zip code is 82496.
   b. My zip code is 91109.

3. Where do you live?
   a. I live at 350 Hudson Avenue, #4A.
   b. I live at Valley Adult School.

4. What is your date of birth?
   a. My date of birth is 91109.
   b. My date of birth is 4-17-1970.

Check your answers. See page 128.

3 Complete the sentences. Fill in the crossword puzzle.

address	country	state
apartment	last	title
city	middle	zip

Down

1. Vietnam is a _____country_____ .

2. Her name is Sue Ling Chang. Ling is

   her _____ name.

4. Her _____ name is Chang.

5. California is a _____ .

8. *Mrs.* is a _____ .

Across

3. The number 91109 is a

   _____ code.

6. Her _____ is 350 Hudson

   Avenue, #4A.

7. Her _____ number is 4A.

9. Pasadena is a _____ .

Check your answers. See page 128.

1 Unscramble the letters. Write the words.

1. laccrlauto _____calculator_____
2. oobk _____
3. pencli _____
4. pma _____
5. bleat _____

6. kcclo _____
7. dkse _____
8. sreear _____
9. koobteno _____
10. rluer _____

2 Look at the picture. Write the words from Exercise 1.

1. _____clock_____
2. _____
3. _____
4. _____
5. _____
6. _____
7. _____
8. _____
9. _____
10. _____

Check your answers. See page 128.

3 Look at the picture in Exercise 2. What's on the desks? What's on the table?

| book | calculator | eraser | notebook | pencil | ruler |

On the desks

_____   _____

_____   _____

On the table

___book___

_____

4 Read the Acme catalog page. Circle the answers.

ACME
OFFICE SUPPLIES

100% GUARANTEE

A   B   C

ITEM	QUANTITY	PRICE
(A) Calculator	1	$4.97
(B) Wall clock	1	$11.48
(C) Clock with radio	1	$49.99
(D) Pencil erasers	12	$4.89
(E) Whiteboard eraser	2	$4.19

D   E

CALL
1-888-555-DESK

418   419

1. What do the calculators cost?
   a. $4.19
   b. $4.89
   c. $4.97

2. What costs $49.99?
   a. the calculator
   b. the clock with radio
   c. the wall clock

3. How many pencil erasers cost $4.89?
   a. 2
   b. 4
   c. 12

4. What is Acme's area code?
   a. 888
   b. 555
   c. 418

Check your answers. See page 128.

At school 15

Where is the pen?

1 Look at the pictures. Write the words. Then circle *in* or *on*.

| calculator | calendar | computer | dictionary | eraser | ruler |

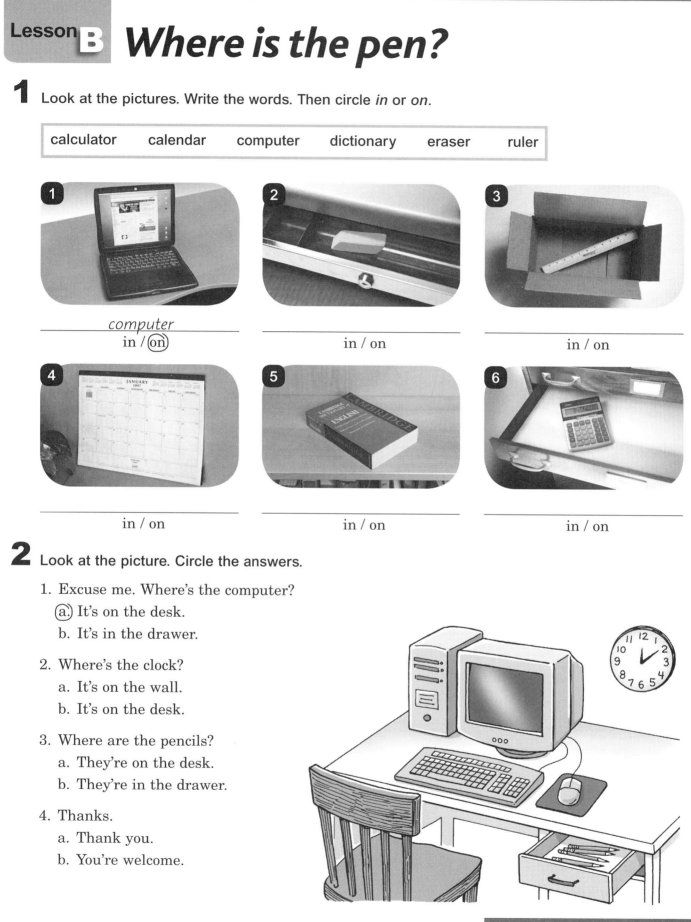

1
computer
in / (on)

2
in / on

3
in / on

4
in / on

5
in / on

6
in / on

2 Look at the picture. Circle the answers.

1. Excuse me. Where's the computer?
   (a.) It's on the desk.
   b. It's in the drawer.

2. Where's the clock?
   a. It's on the wall.
   b. It's on the desk.

3. Where are the pencils?
   a. They're on the desk.
   b. They're in the drawer.

4. Thanks.
   a. Thank you.
   b. You're welcome.

Check your answers. See page 128.

3 Look at the picture. Write questions and answers.

1. calculators

   A *Where are the calculators?*

   B *They're on the table.*

2. calendar

   A _____

   B _____

3. books

   A _____

   B _____

4. notebook

   A _____

   B _____

4 Number the sentences in the correct order.

_____ On the shelf?

_____ Thank you.

_1_ Excuse me. Where's the dictionary?

_____ You're welcome.

_____ Yes. It's on the shelf.

_____ It's on the shelf.

5 Write questions and answers. Use *in* or *on*.

1. A *Where's the pencil?*
   (pencil)

   B *It's on the table.*
   (table)

2. A _____
   (calendar)

   B _____
   (wall)

3. A _____
   (eraser)

   B _____
   (desk)

4. A _____
   (ruler)

   B _____
   (box)

5. A _____
   (calculator)

   B _____
   (drawer)

6. A _____
   (pen)

   B _____
   (table)

Check your answers. See page 128.

Where are the pencils?

1 Look at the pictures. Write the words.

| bookcase | desks | dictionary | erasers | notebooks | pencils | rulers |

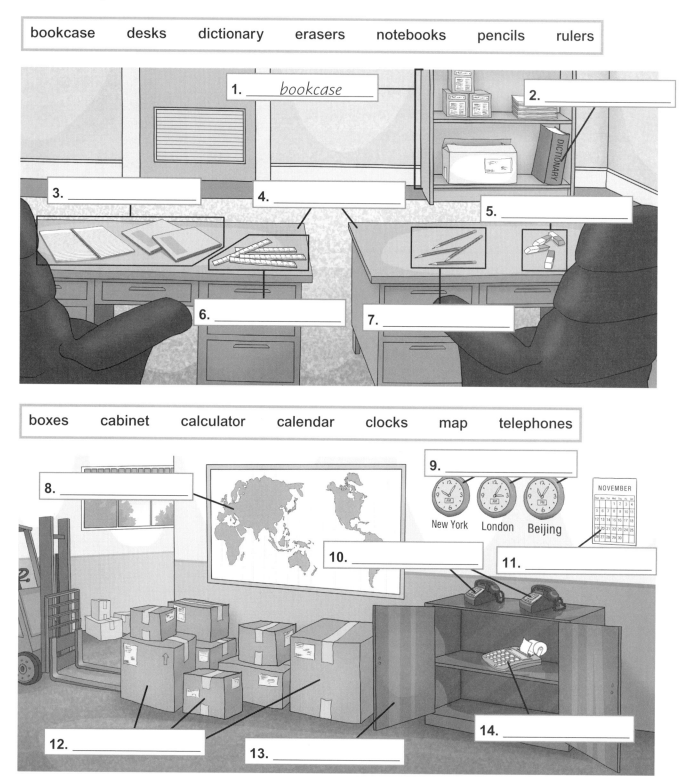

1. _bookcase_
2. _____
3. _____
4. _____
5. _____
6. _____
7. _____

| boxes | cabinet | calculator | calendar | clocks | map | telephones |

8. _____
9. _____
10. _____
11. _____
12. _____
13. _____
14. _____

NOVEMBER

New York   London   Beijing

Check your answers. See page 128.

2 Complete the charts. Use the words from Exercise 1.

Singular nouns	
bookcase	

Plural nouns	

3 Complete the sentences. Use *it is*, *it isn't*, *they are*, or *they aren't*.

1. **A** Are the calendars on the table?

   B Yes, _____they are_____ .

2. **A** Is the ruler in the box?

   B No, _____ .

3. **A** Are the bookcases in the classroom?

   B Yes, _____ .

4. **A** Is the eraser on the teacher's desk?

   B Yes, _____ .

5. **A** Are the maps on the wall?

   B No, _____ .

6. **A** Is the pencil in the drawer?

   B No, _____ .

7. **A** Are the dictionaries in the bookcase?

   B Yes, _____ .

8. **A** Are the boxes on the filing cabinet?

   B Yes, _____ .

9. **A** Is his notebook on the desk?

   B No, _____ .

10. **A** Are the calculators on the table?

    B Yes, _____ .

4 Write sentences.

1. **A** Where / the dictionaries / are / ?

   _Where are the dictionaries?_____

   B are / They / on / the shelf / .

   _____

2. **A** the book / on / Is / the table / ?

   _____

   B isn't / No, / it / .

   _____

3. **A** Is / the desk drawer / the pencil / in / ?

   _____

   B it / Yes, / is / .

   _____

Check your answers. See page 128.

Reading

1 Find the words.

cabinet	computer	eraser	notebook	rulers
chalkboard	dictionaries	globe	notepad	stapler

```
s  d  n  o  t  e  p  a  d (c) e
e  a  o  c  l  u  r  d  i  o  m
r  n  s  p  e  e  g  a  c  m  s
t  u (c  a  b  i  n  e  t) p  l
e  r  a  e  l  a  o  t  i  u  e
d  d  r  s  k  t  t  g  o  t  t
c  s  t  o  o  e  l  n  e  o
d  c  h  a  l  k  b  o  a  r  d
p  o  l  p  a  a  o  b  r  a  l
b  c  p  l  o  r  o  e  i  s  l
s  a  d  e  b  u  k  m  e  e  l
d  m  u  r  u  l  e  r  s  r  b
```

2 Match the questions with the answers.

1. Are the index cards on the top shelf? _f_

2. Is the chalk in the box? ____

3. Is the ruler on the table? ____

4. Are the dictionaries in the cabinet? ____

5. Is the notebook in the drawer? ____

6. Is the stapler on the desk? ____

a. No, they aren't. The dictionaries are on the table.

b. No, it isn't. The chalk is in the cabinet.

c. No, it isn't. The stapler is in the cabinet.

d. Yes, it's in the drawer.

e. Yes, it's on the table.

f. No, they aren't. The index cards are on the bottom shelf.

Check your answers. See page 129.

3 Write a conversation. Use the sentences in the box.

Speaker A	Speaker B
The notebooks are on the top shelf.	Thanks. I also need a pencil.
May I help you?	Great. Now I'm ready to write!
Pencils are on the bottom shelf.	Yes, please. Where are the notebooks?

1. **A** _May I help you?_ _____
2. **B** _____
3. **A** _____
4. **B** _____
5. **A** _____
6. **B** _____

4 Read the letter. Answer the questions.

acme

July 6, 2007

Dear Ang,

Welcome to Acme Offices! The notepads are in the desk drawer. The pencils are in a box on the shelf. The erasers are in the box, too. The dictionaries are in the bookcase. The stapler is on the desk.

Sincerely,
Mrs. Grant
Manager

1. Where are the notepads? _The notepads are in the desk drawer._ _____
2. Where are the pencils? _____
3. Where are the erasers? _____
4. Where are the dictionaries? _____
5. Where's the stapler? _____

Check your answers. See page 129.

Lesson E *Writing*

1 Write sentences.

1. Where / the / books / are / ?

   Where are the books?

2. The pencil sharpener / is / the wall / on / .

   _____

3. the books / Are / the shelf / on / ?

   _____

4. are / The pencils / the desk / on / .

   _____

5. the teacher / the classroom / Is / in / ?

   _____

6. is / the computer / Where / ?

   _____

7. The notebook / the desk / on / is / .

   _____

8. in / the drawer / Is / the stapler / ?

   _____

Check your answers. See page 129.

2 Circle the correct words.

1. A Is the map on the wall?
   B Yes, (it is)/ they are.

2. A Are the pens in the box?
   B No, it isn't / they aren't.

3. A Is the notebook on the table?
   B Yes, it is / they are.

4. A Are the calculators in the drawer?
   B Yes, it is / they are.

5. A Is the ruler on the desk?
   B No, it isn't / they aren't.

6. A Is the computer on the table?
   B Yes, it is / they are.

7. A Are the desks in the classroom?
   B Yes, it is / they are.

8. A Is the chalkboard on the wall?
   B Yes, it is / they are.

9. A Is the dictionary on the desk?
   B No, it isn't / they aren't.

3 Correct the sentences. Add capital letters and periods. Then rewrite the correct sentences.

1. T̶the classroom is ready for the students.

2. the books are in the bookcase

3. the map is on the wall

4. the globe is on the filing cabinet

5. the pencils are on the table

6. the teacher's name is on the chalkboard

7. the markers are in the drawer

8. the calculators are on the bookcase

1. _The classroom is ready for the students._

2. _____

3. _____

4. _____

5. _____

6. _____

7. _____

8. _____

Check your answers. See page 129.

Another view

1 Read the questions. Look at the chart. Circle the answers.

ITEM	QUANTITY	LOCATION
notebook	15	in the cabinet
computer	3	on the desks
calculator	1	on the table
ruler	2	on the teacher's desk
dictionary	30	in the bookcase
pencil	5	in the cabinet
book	30	in the bookcase

1. Where are the notebooks?
   a. in the cabinet
   b. in the drawer
   c. on the desk
   d. on the bookcase

2. What are on the desks?
   a. notebooks
   b. computers
   c. dictionaries
   d. pencils

3. What's in the bookcase?
   a. a computer
   b. dictionaries and books
   c. notebooks and pencils
   d. a ruler

4. How many computers are on the desks?
   a. 1
   b. 2
   c. 3
   d. 5

5. What's in the cabinet?
   a. notebooks and computers
   b. rulers and dictionaries
   c. books and rulers
   d. notebooks and pencils

6. What's on the table?
   a. a book
   b. a computer
   c. a notebook
   d. a calculator

7. Where are the dictionaries?
   a. in the bookcase
   b. in the cabinet
   c. in the desks
   d. on the table

8. How many notebooks are in the cabinet?
   a. 3
   b. 5
   c. 15
   d. 30

Check your answers. See page 129.

2 Complete the puzzle.

Down

1  3

5  6

7 8

Across

2 4

9 10

11

Check your answers. See page 129.

Lesson A Get ready

1 Look at the picture. Write the words.

| brother | father | grandfather | grandmother | mother | sister |

Esteban

1. _grandfather_

Consuela

2. _____

Sylvia

3. _____

Luis

4. _____

Andrea

5. _____

Jorge

6. _____

2 Complete the sentences.

| daughter | grandfather | mother | son | wife |

Family Photo

This is a picture of my family. Sheila is my

_____wife_____ . In front of her are James, our
1.

_____ , and Megan, our _____ .
2.   3.

Behind Sheila are her _____
                                    4.

and father. Megan and James love their

_____ and grandmother very much!
5.

Check your answers. See page 129.

3 Read the phone list. Answer the questions.

Emergency: 911

Coach Jones (Luis's basketball coach):
(973) 555-1972

Grandmother and Grandfather:
(808) 555-8221
711F 7th Avenue, Honolulu, HI 96816

Jefferson Elementary (Luis's school):
(973) 555-1920
59 Concord Road, West Milford, NJ, 07480

Mrs. Chen (Sylvia's piano teacher):
(973) 555-1766

Mrs. Bosch (Mother's art teacher):
(201) 555-1850

Superior Textbooks (Father's work):
(212) 555-1234
40 West 20th Street, New York, NY 10011

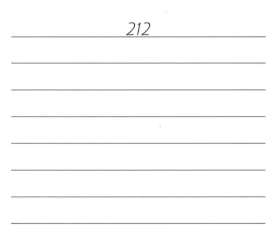

1. What is the area code for Superior Textbooks?   _____212_____

2. What is the zip code for Jefferson Elementary?   _____

3. What is the telephone number for Mrs. Bosch?   _____

4. What is the last name of Sylvia's piano teacher? _____

5. What is the telephone number for Coach Jones?   _____

6. Where do the grandmother and grandfather live? _____

7. What is the last name of Luis's basketball coach? _____

8. What is the address for Superior Textbooks?   _____

Check your answers. See page 129.

What are you doing?

Study the chart on page 122.

1 Read the chart. Answer the questions.

> *Jason's Chores - Saturday*
> *9 a.m. Clean room*
> *10 a.m. Study English*
> *11 a.m. Help Dad*
> *1 p.m. Watch little sister*
> *9 p.m. Wash dishes*

1. It's 9:00 a.m. What is Jason doing?   *He's cleaning his room.*

2. It's 10:00 a.m. What is Jason doing?   _____

3. It's 11:00 a.m. What is Jason doing?   _____

4. It's 1:00 p.m. What is Jason doing?   _____

5. It's 9:00 p.m. What is Jason doing?   _____

2 Complete the sentences.

1. **A** What's Mimi doing?

   B She *'s cleaning* the house.
   (clean)

2. **A** What's Hsu-jing doing?

   B She _____ on the phone.
   (talk)

3. **A** What's Anatoly doing?

   B He _____ on the beach.
   (play)

4. **A** What's Irene doing?

   B She _____ lunch.
   (eat)

5. **A** What's Pierre doing?

   B He _____ TV.
   (watch)

6. **A** What's Brenda doing?

   B She _____ to music.
   (listen)

7. **A** What's Louis doing?

   B He _____ English.
   (study)

8. **A** What's Ibrahim doing?

   B He _____ tea.
   (drink)

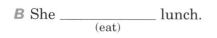
Check your answers. See page 129.

3 Read the story. Circle the present continuous verbs.

Mother's Day

Today is Mother's Day. The whole family (is celebrating) Mom's hard work. This morning, Mom is sleeping. Dad is cooking a big breakfast for Mom. Salvatore is cleaning the house. His sister, Isabella, is helping Dad.

Mom,
Thanks for being the best.
Love,
Isabella, Salvatore, and Dad

4 Write a conversation. Use the sentences in the box.

Speaker A	Speaker B
I'm OK. What are you doing?	Hi, Margie. How are you?
Hello?	I'm taking a break. Are you busy?
They're doing their homework.	What are the children doing?
Yes, I'm cooking dinner.	That's good. See you soon.

1. A *Hello?*

2. B _____

3. A _____

4. B _____

5. A _____

6. B _____

7. A _____

8. B _____

Check your answers. See page 129.

Study the chart on page 122.

1 Look at the picture. Answer the questions.

1. Is Rachel cleaning the house?   *Yes, she is.*
2. Is Todd studying?   _____
3. Is Tim watching TV?   _____
4. Is David reading a newspaper?   _____
5. Is Brooke listening to music?   _____
6. Is Tim talking on the phone?   _____
7. Are they eating dinner?   _____
8. Are they having a party?   _____

2 Look at the picture in Exercise 1. Answer the questions.

1. What is Rachel doing?   *She is cleaning the house.*
2. What is Brooke doing?   _____
3. What is Tim doing?   _____
4. What is David doing?   _____
5. What is Todd doing?   _____

Check your answers. See page 130.

3 Change the answers in Exercise 2 into questions.

1. _Is she cleaning the house?_ _____

2. _____

3. _____

4. _____

5. _____

4 Look at the pictures. Complete the sentences.

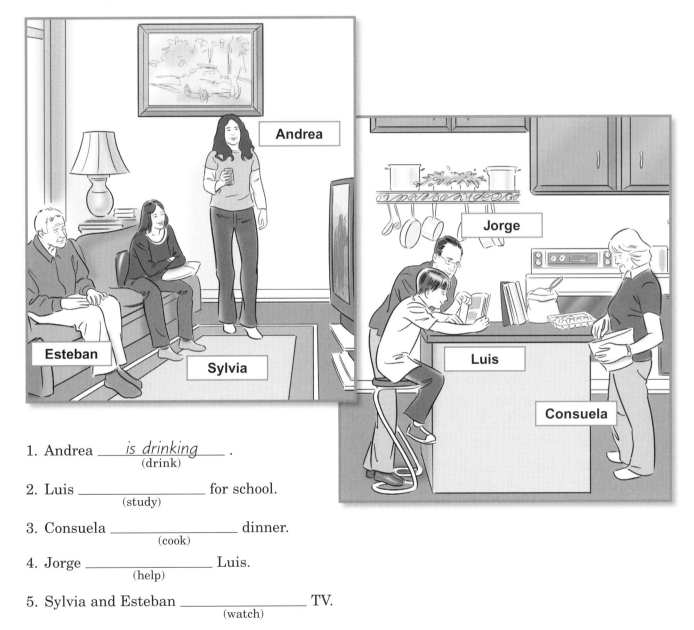

1. Andrea ____is drinking____ .
       (drink)

2. Luis _____ for school.
         (study)

3. Consuela _____ dinner.
              (cook)

4. Jorge _____ Luis.
            (help)

5. Sylvia and Esteban _____ TV.
                         (watch)

Check your answers. See page 130.

1 Read the story. Write the names on the family tree.

> Javid is married to Sara. They have two children, one son and one daughter. The son's name is Omid, and the daughter's name is Avid. Omid is married to Leila. They have two sons, Daniel and Ali. Avid isn't married. She doesn't have any children.

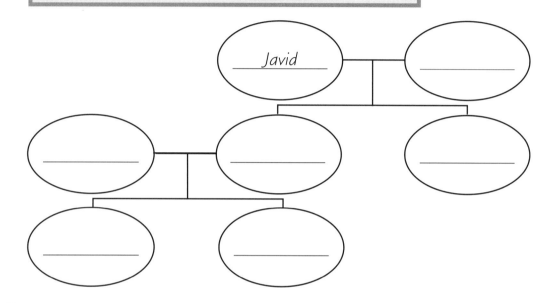

Javid

2 Read the questions. Complete the answers.

brother	grandfather	grandson	mother	son
daughter	grandmother	husband	sister	wife

1. Who is Javid? He is Sara's _____husband_____ .

2. Who is Sara? She is Avid's _____ .

3. Who is Leila? She is Omid's _____ .

4. Who is Avid? She is Omid's _____ .

5. Who is Omid? He is Avid's _____ .

6. Who is Ali? He is Javid's _____ .

7. Who is Avid? She is Javid's _____ .

8. Who is Omid? He is Sara's _____ .

9. Who is Javid? He is Daniel's _____ .

10. Who is Sara? She is Ali's _____ .

Check your answers. See page 130.

3 Complete the sentences.

| cousin | grandmother | niece | sister-in-law |
| grandfather | nephew | sister | uncle |

1. My mother's mother is my _____ *grandmother* _____ .

2. My mother's father is my _____ .

3. My brother's wife is my _____ .

4. My mother's brother is my _____ .

5. My father's daughter is my _____ .

6. My brother's daughter is my _____ .

7. My sister's son is my _____ .

8. My aunt's daughter is my _____ .

4 Write a conversation. Use the sentences in the box.

Speaker A	Speaker B
Don't worry. It isn't a big test.	Hi, Susan. This is Ann. What are you doing?
I'm studying for the English test.	That's good. Talk to you later.
Hello? This is Susan.	Oh, no! I forgot about the test.
OK. See you tomorrow, Ann.	

1. **A** *Hello? This is Susan.* _____

2. **B** _____

   _____

3. **A** _____

   _____

4. **B** _____

   _____

5. **A** _____

   _____

6. **B** _____

   _____

7. **A** _____

   _____

Check your answers. See page 130.

1 Write sentences.

1. **A** doing / What / you / are / ?

   What are you doing?

   B family / cooking for / my / I'm / .

   _____

2. **A** brothers / How many / do / have / you / ?

   _____

   B two / I / brothers / have / .

   _____

3. **A** you / Do / any sisters / have / ?

   _____

   B have / I / sisters / five / .

   _____

2 Correct the sentences. Add capital letters.

1. T̶oday is Ana's birthday.

2. she is 15 years old.

3. ana's mother, luisa, is making a birthday cake.

4. her grandparents are wrapping presents.

5. ana is having a big party.

6. her friends are dancing at the party.

7. ana's father, reynaldo, is taking pictures.

8. they are very happy today.

Check your answers. See page 130.

3 Complete the sentences.

1. **A** What are you doing?

   B _We're having_ a party. It's Paul's birthday.
      (we / have)

2. **A** Who's there?

   B Well, Sally and Jim are here. _____ .
      (they / talk)

3. **A** Who else is there?

   B Frank and Jane are here. _____ now.
      (they / sing)

4. **A** Is Mother there?

   B Yes, Mother is here. _____ dinner now.
      (she / cook)

5. **A** What is Paul doing?

   B _____ pictures.
      (he / take)

4 Read the sentences. Then rewrite them. Change *Paul* (a boy) to *Paula* (a girl).

1. I am married. I have one son.
2. His name is Paul.
3. He is 10 years old today.
4. He is having a party with his friends.
5. Paul and his friends are playing outside now.
6. He is happy.

1. _I am married. I have one daughter._
2. _____
3. _____
4. _____
5. _____
6. _____

Check your answers. See page 130.

Another view

1 Complete Luis's family tree.

| aunt | cousin | father | grandfather | grandmother | mother | sister | uncle |

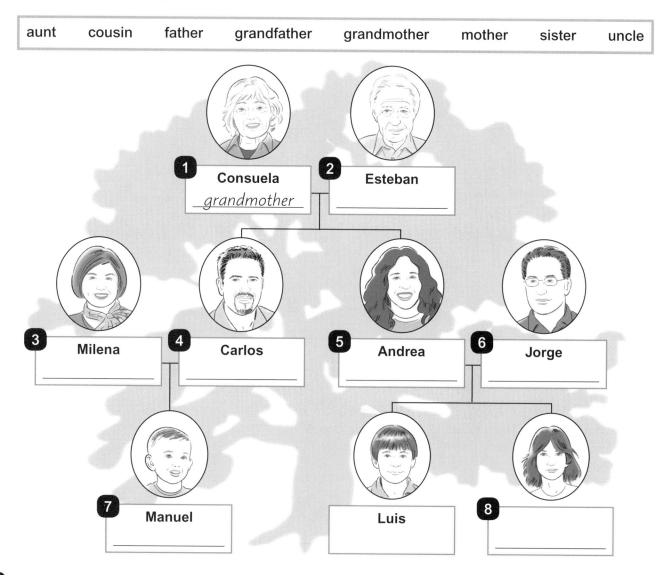

1 Consuela
grandmother

2 Esteban
_____

3 Milena
_____

4 Carlos
_____

5 Andrea
_____

6 Jorge
_____

7 Manuel
_____

Luis

8
_____

2 Look at the bold word. Cross out the word that is different.

1. **mother** ~~son~~ sister grandmother
2. **cooking** cleaning daughter studying
3. **niece** nephew birthday aunt
4. **brother** grandfather uncle watching
5. **reading** listening playing music
6. **book** dictionary newspaper TV
7. **drinking** eating guitar watching
8. **husband** wife daughter friend

Check your answers. See page 130.

3 Look at the tax form. Circle the answers.

Form 1			Tax Form 2007

Form 1 — **Tax Form 2007**

First Name: Duc
Last Name: Nguyen

Exemptions
a. Yourself ☒
b. Spouse ☒

Dependents

First name	Last name	Social Security Number	Relationship
Lam	Nguyen	555-93-2458	daughter
Thanh	Nguyen	555-84-3498	son
Toan	Nguyen	555-52-1256	daughter
Lien	Le	555-32-3421	mother

No. of children who live with you 3

Total number of exemptions claimed 6

1020 EZ

1. How many daughters does Duc have?
   a. 1
   b. 2 *(circled)*
   c. 3

2. How many children live with Duc?
   a. 2
   b. 3
   c. 4

3. Who are Duc's dependents?
   a. his son
   b. his daughters
   c. his mother, son, and daughters

4. How many sons does Duc have?
   a. 1
   b. 2
   c. 3

4 Read the birth certificate. Answer the questions.

Certificate of Birth
First General Hospital
Chicago

Petra Clarkson, *female*
Born: *June 2, 2006*
Mother: *Bianca Martinez Clarkson*
Father: *Josh Clarkson*

1. Where is the hospital? _Chicago_

2. What is the family's last name? _____

3. What is the mother's first name? _____

4. What is Petra's birthday? _____

Check your answers. See page 130.

1 Find the words.

ache	back	cough	fever	sore
ankle	cold	ear	head	stomach

```
a   n   k   l   e   a   e   a   r
s   o   r   e   t   k   c   c   m
t   s   r   a   h   t   o   h   s
f   e   v   e   r   b   u   e   n
o   a   e   d   o   a   g   h   h
s   t   o   m   a   c   h   t   e
a   t   h   k   t   k   r   a   a
a   t   e   a   s   e   e   d   d
s   c   o   l   d   s   c   f   o
```

2 Complete the chart. Use the words from Exercise 1.

Parts of the body	Problems
ankle	*ache*

3 Match the words.

1. sore   _c_   a. ankle

2. head   ____   b. leg

3. sprained   ____   c. throat

4. broken   ____   d. ache

Check your answers. See page 130.

4 Look at the pictures. Write the words.

backache	earache	sore throat
broken leg	fever	sprained ankle
cough	headache	stomachache

headache

Check your answers. See page 131.

I have a headache.

Study the chart on page 124.

1 Read the flyer. Circle the answers.

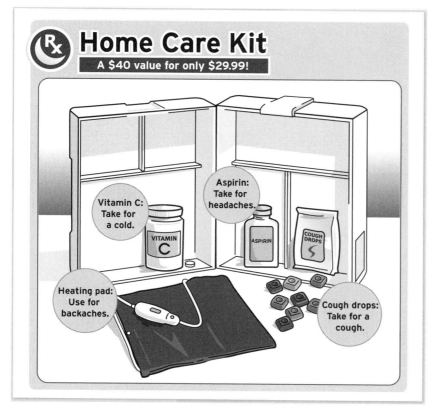

1. What do you take for a cough?
   a. aspirin
   b. a heating pad
   (c.) cough drops
   d. vitamin C

2. What do you take for headaches?
   a. aspirin
   b. a heating pad
   c. cough drops
   d. vitamin C

3. What do you use for a backache?
   a. aspirin
   b. a heating pad
   c. cough drops
   d. vitamin C

4. What do you take for a cold?
   a. aspirin
   b. a heating pad
   c. cough drops
   d. vitamin C

2 Complete the sentences. Use *have* or *has*.

1. They ___have___ colds.

2. She _____ a fever.

3. He _____ a cough.

4. I _____ a sore throat.

5. They _____ headaches.

6. You _____ a broken arm.

Check your answers. See page 131.

3 Answer the questions.

1 A What's wrong?

B _He has a broken arm._

2 A What's wrong?

B _____

3 A What's wrong?

B _____

4 A What's wrong?

B _____

5 A What's wrong?

B _____

6 A What's wrong?

B _____

4 Write a conversation. Use the sentences in the box.

Speaker A	Speaker B
Yes, I do. I have aspirin and vitamin C.	I'm tired, and I'm hot.
How are you?	Yes, I do. Do you have aspirin?
Do you have a fever?	Thank you.

1. A _How are you?_

2. B _____

_____

3. A _____

_____

4. B _____

_____

5. A _____

_____

6. B _____

_____

Check your answers. See page 131.

Lesson C *Do you have a cold?*

Study the chart on page 124.

1 Circle the answers.

1. What's wrong?
   a. My daughter has a fever.
   b. My daughter have a fever.

2. Does she have a backache?
   a. No, she doesn't.
   b. No, she don't.

3. Does she have an earache?
   a. Yes, she do.
   b. Yes, she does.

4. Does she have a sore throat?
   a. No, she don't.
   b. No, she doesn't.

5. Do you have a stomachache?
   a. No, I don't.
   b. No, I do.

2 Complete the sentences.

Kenji is sick. He ___*has*___ the flu. _____ has a sore throat and a
      1. has / have   2. He / His

cough. He _____ have a backache. Kenji also _____ a headache.
           3. doesn't / don't   4. has / have

He _____ have any medicine. He _____ have a doctor.
     5. do / doesn't   6. do / does

3 Complete the sentences.

1. **A** John isn't at work today.
   B Oh. What's wrong with ___*him*___ ?
   A ___*He*___ has a fever and a cold.
   B That's too bad.

2. **A** Annie isn't at school today.
   B Oh. What's wrong with _____ ?
   A _____ has a cold.
   B I'm sorry.

3. **A** My husband isn't at work today.
   B Oh. What's wrong with _____ ?
   A _____ has a broken arm.
   B I hope he feels better.

4. **A** My daughter isn't at school today.
   B Oh. What's wrong with _____ ?
   A _____ has a very bad headache.
   B That's too bad.

Check your answers. See page 131.

4 Write questions.

1. a stomachache

   A *Does she have a stomachache?*

   B No, she doesn't. She has a headache.

2. a sore throat

   A _____

   B Yes, he does.

3. a broken leg

   A _____

   B No, he doesn't. He has a sore ankle.

4. colds

   A _____

   B No, they don't. They have sore throats.

5. a cough

   A _____

   B No, I don't. I have a sore throat.

6. a fever

   A _____

   B Yes, I do.

7. an earache

   A _____

   B Yes, she does.

8. a cut

   A _____

   B No, I don't. I have the flu.

9. a sprained ankle

   A _____

   B No, she doesn't. She has a broken leg.

10. headaches

    A _____

    B Yes, they do.

Check your answers. See page 131.

1 Unscramble the letters. Write the words.

1. eot   <u> *toe* </u>
2. neso   <u>   </u>
3. lekan   <u>   </u>
4. yee   <u>   </u>

5. nich   <u>   </u>
6. nahd   <u>   </u>
7. iregnf   <u>   </u>
8. otof   <u>   </u>

9. ekne   <u>   </u>
10. tohot   <u>   </u>
11. rea   <u>   </u>
12. stmchao   <u>   </u>

2 Complete the sentences. Use the words from Exercise 1.

1 His <u> *eye* </u> hurts.

2 Her <u>   </u> hurts.

3 His <u>   </u> hurts.

4 His <u>   </u> hurts.

5 Her <u>   </u> hurts.

6 Her <u>   </u> hurts.

Check your answers. See page 131.

3 Number the sentences in the correct order. Then write the conversation below.

___ Hi, Ms. Jones. I'm not so good.

___ Thank you.

___ My knee hurts. I have a cut.

_1_ Good morning, Jamie. How are you today?

___ I'm sorry. Here. Use this bandage.

___ What's wrong?

Ms. Jones _Good morning, Jamie. How are you today?_

Jamie _____

Ms. Jones _____

Jamie _____

Ms. Jones _____

Jamie _____

4 Read the story. Answer the questions.

> The Simon family is at the doctor's office. Their 12-year-old son, Bobby, has a sore arm. Their six-year-old daughter, Margaret, has a cold and a sore throat. Their baby girl has a fever and a cough. Mr. and Mrs. Simon are tired!

1. Where is the Simon family?

   The Simon family is at the doctor's office.

2. What's the matter with Bobby?

   _____

3. What's wrong with Margaret?

   _____

4. Does the baby have a fever?

   _____

5. How are Mr. and Mrs. Simon feeling?

   _____

Check your answers. See page 131.

1 Look at the note. Circle the items.

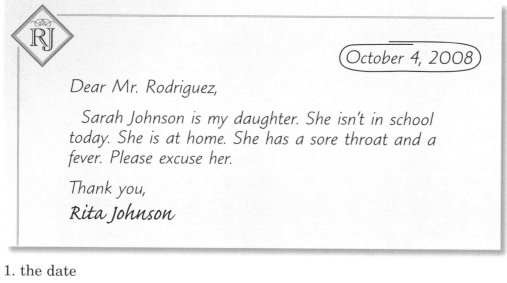

October 4, 2008

Dear Mr. Rodriguez,

Sarah Johnson is my daughter. She isn't in school today. She is at home. She has a sore throat and a fever. Please excuse her.

Thank you,
Rita Johnson

1. the date
2. the teacher's name
3. the name of the sick child
4. what's wrong
5. the signature

2 Correct the note. Add capital letters.

April 14, 2008

D
dear miss nguyen,

debra garcia is my niece. she isn't in school today. she is at home. she has a cold and a fever. please excuse her.

thank you,
Jerry Garcia

Check your answers. See page 131.

3 Rewrite the note from Mr. Garcia. Change *Debra* (a girl) to *Jim* (a boy).

> October 4, 2008
>
> Dear Miss Nguyen,
>
> Jim Garcia is my nephew. _____
>
> _____
>
> _____
>
> _____
>
> _____
>
> Thank you,
>
> *Jerry Garcia*

4 Number the sentences in the correct order. Then write the note.

____ Thank you,

    Tom Jones

____ He has a fever and a cough. Please excuse him.

_1_ January 21, 2008

____ Barry Jones is my son. He isn't in school today.

____ Dear Ms. Adams,

____ He is at home.

Check your answers. See page 131.

Another view

1 Complete the chart.

ankle	chin	finger	head	neck	stomach	tooth
arm	ear	foot	knee	nose	throat	wrist
back	eye	hand	leg	shoulder	toe	

How many does a person have?		
One	**A pair (two)**	**More than two**
	ankle	

2 Complete the sentences.

cough	fever	sore throat
earache	headache	stomachache

1. He isn't eating. He has a _____stomachache_____ .

2. She is taking cough drops. She has a _____ .

3. The teacher isn't talking today. He has a _____ .

4. I'm taking aspirin. I'm hot. I have a _____ .

5. My head hurts. I have a _____ .

6. My ear hurts. I have an _____ .

Check your answers. See page 131.

3 Look at the appointment card. Answer the questions.

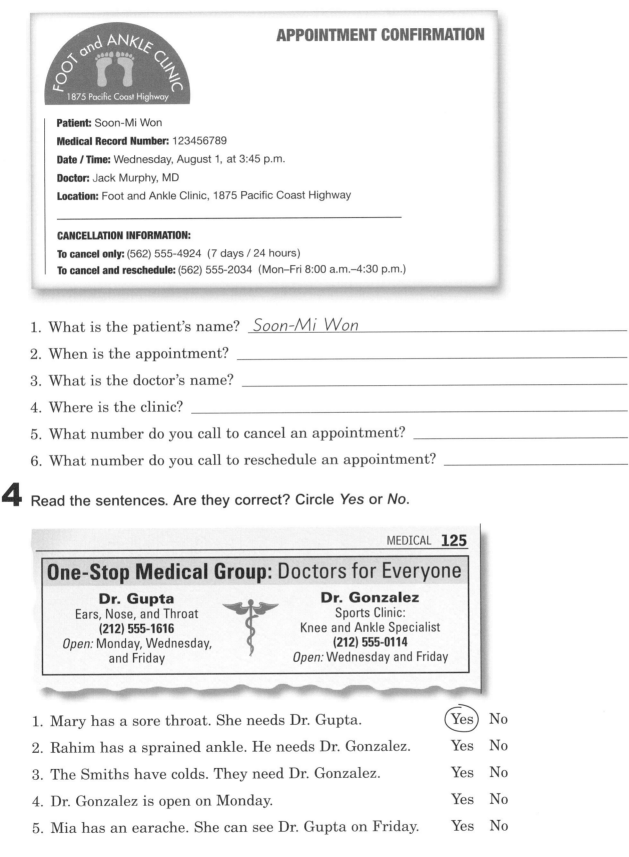

APPOINTMENT CONFIRMATION

FOOT and ANKLE CLINIC
1875 Pacific Coast Highway

Patient: Soon-Mi Won
Medical Record Number: 123456789
Date / Time: Wednesday, August 1, at 3:45 p.m.
Doctor: Jack Murphy, MD
Location: Foot and Ankle Clinic, 1875 Pacific Coast Highway

CANCELLATION INFORMATION:
To cancel only: (562) 555-4924 (7 days / 24 hours)
To cancel and reschedule: (562) 555-2034 (Mon–Fri 8:00 a.m.–4:30 p.m.)

1. What is the patient's name? _Soon-Mi Won_
2. When is the appointment? _____
3. What is the doctor's name? _____
4. Where is the clinic? _____
5. What number do you call to cancel an appointment? _____
6. What number do you call to reschedule an appointment? _____

4 Read the sentences. Are they correct? Circle *Yes* or *No*.

MEDICAL **125**

One-Stop Medical Group: Doctors for Everyone

Dr. Gupta
Ears, Nose, and Throat
(212) 555-1616
Open: Monday, Wednesday,
and Friday

Dr. Gonzalez
Sports Clinic:
Knee and Ankle Specialist
(212) 555-0114
Open: Wednesday and Friday

1. Mary has a sore throat. She needs Dr. Gupta.   (Yes) No
2. Rahim has a sprained ankle. He needs Dr. Gonzalez.   Yes No
3. The Smiths have colds. They need Dr. Gonzalez.   Yes No
4. Dr. Gonzalez is open on Monday.   Yes No
5. Mia has an earache. She can see Dr. Gupta on Friday.   Yes No

Check your answers. See page 132.

Lesson A Get ready

1 Write the places.

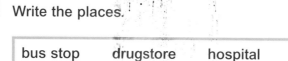

| bus stop | drugstore | hospital | restaurant |

1. Eat here: *restaurant*

2. See a doctor here: _____

3. Get the bus here: _____

4. Buy medicine here: _____

2 Complete the sentences.

| grocery store | hospital | library | museum |

1. The _____*museum*_____ has paintings.

2. My grandmother is sick. She is in the _____ .

3. We read books at the _____ .

4. We're buying groceries at the _____ .

Check your answers. See page 132.

3 Look at the pictures. Write the places.

bus stop	grocery store	house	museum	restaurant
drugstore	hospital	library	post office	

1. _restaurant_

2. _____

3. _____

4. _____

5. _____

6. _____

7. _____

8. _____

9. _____

4 What places are these? Write the words.

hospital	library	restaurant	school

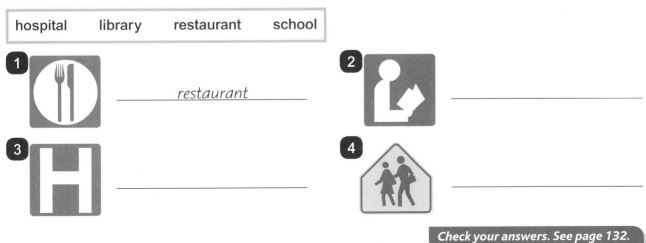

1. _restaurant_

2. _____

3. _____

4. _____

Check your answers. See page 132.

It's on the corner.

1 Look at the map. Complete the sentences.

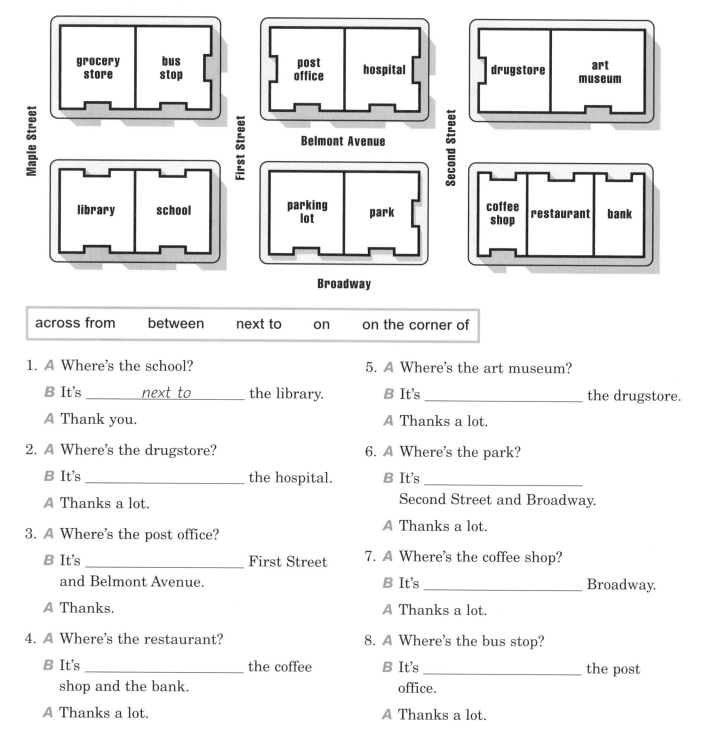

across from	between	next to	on	on the corner of

1. **A** Where's the school?

   B It's _____*next to*_____ the library.

   A Thank you.

2. **A** Where's the drugstore?

   B It's _____ the hospital.

   A Thanks a lot.

3. **A** Where's the post office?

   B It's _____ First Street and Belmont Avenue.

   A Thanks.

4. **A** Where's the restaurant?

   B It's _____ the coffee shop and the bank.

   A Thanks a lot.

5. **A** Where's the art museum?

   B It's _____ the drugstore.

   A Thanks a lot.

6. **A** Where's the park?

   B It's _____ Second Street and Broadway.

   A Thanks a lot.

7. **A** Where's the coffee shop?

   B It's _____ Broadway.

   A Thanks a lot.

8. **A** Where's the bus stop?

   B It's _____ the post office.

   A Thanks a lot.

Check your answers. See page 132.

2 Look at the map in Exercise 1. Answer the questions.

1. Where's the drugstore?

   It's on the corner of Belmont Avenue and Second Street.
                                      (on the corner of)

2. Where's the art museum?

   _____
                                      (on)

3. Where's the post office?

   _____
                                      (next to)

4. Where's the hospital?

   _____
                                      (on the corner of)

5. Where's the school?

   _____
                                      (next to)

6. Where's the bank?

   _____
                                      (on)

7. Where's the bus stop?

   _____
                                      (across from)

8. Where's the restaurant?

   _____
                                      (between)

9. Where's the grocery store?

   _____
                                      (on the corner of)

10. Where's the library?

   _____
                                      (across from)

3 Look at the map in Exercise 1. Write questions.

1. _Where's the school?_   It's next to the library.

2. _____ It's on Belmont Avenue, next to the post office.

3. _____ It's on Broadway, next to the park.

4. _____ It's across from the school.

5. _____ It's on the corner of Maple Street and Broadway.

6. _____ It's next to the drugstore.

7. _____ It's across from the library.

8. _____ It's on Belmont Avenue, between the coffee shop and the bank.

Check your answers. See page 132.

Lesson C Go two blocks.

1 Look at the map. Complete the sentences.

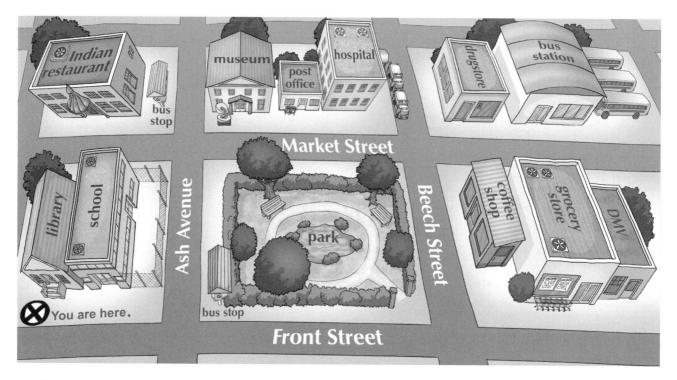

1. Go straight on Front Street. Turn left on Ash Avenue. Turn right on Market Street. Go straight. The ____post office____ is between the museum and the hospital.

2. Go straight on Front Street. Turn left on Ash Avenue. Turn right on Market Street. Go straight. The _____ is on the corner of Beech Street, across from the park.

3. Go straight on Front Street. Cross Ash Avenue, and cross Beech Street. The _____ is on the left, between the coffee shop and the DMV.

4. Go straight two blocks on Front Street. Turn left on Beech Street. Turn right on Market Street. The _____ is on the left, next to the drugstore.

5. Go straight two blocks on Front Street. The _____ is on the left, on the corner of Beech and Front Streets. It's across from the coffee shop.

Check your answers. See page 132.

2 Read the directions. Look at the map in Exercise 1. Write the places.

 Go straight two blocks on Front Street. It's on the corner of Front and Beech Streets, next to the grocery store.

coffee shop

 Go straight on Front Street. Turn left on Ash Avenue. Go one block. Turn left on Market Street. It's next to the bus stop.

_____

 Go straight on Front Street. Turn left on Ash Avenue. Turn right on Market Street. It's on your left, between the museum and the hospital.

_____

 Go straight two blocks on Front Street. Turn left on Beech Street. Turn right on Market Street. It's next to the drugstore.

_____

 Go straight on Front Street. Turn left on Ash Avenue. Go one block. Turn right on Market Street. Go straight. It's on the corner of Market and Beech Streets.

_____

 Go straight on Front Street. Turn left on Ash Avenue. Go one block. Turn right on Market Street. It's on your left, across from the park.

_____

 Go straight on Front Street. Cross Ash Avenue. It's on your left, next to the bus stop.

_____

Check your answers. See page 132.

1 Complete the chart.

coffee shop	grocery store	hospital	police station
day-care center	high school	playground	restaurant

Places for children	Places for food	Places for help
day-care center		

2 Complete the sentences.

apartment building	day-care center	high school	hospital	shopping mall

1. There aren't any houses in her neighborhood, but there's a big _apartment building_ .
2. Mrs. Won is teaching at the _____ now.
3. The _____ has many different stores.
4. Stella is taking her sick daughter to the _____ .
5. Katia is driving her three-year-old son to the _____ .

3 Write a conversation. Use the sentences in the box

Speaker A	Speaker B
It's on the corner of Sixth and Union?	It's on the corner of Fifth and Union.
Excuse me, where's the post office?	Yes, it's next to the bank.
OK, Fifth and Union. Is it next to the bank?	No, on Fifth and Union.

1. A *Excuse me, where's the post office?* _____
2. B _____
3. A _____
4. B _____
5. A _____
6. B _____

Check your answers. See page 132.

4 Read the postcard. Answer the questions.

> January 14, 2008
>
> Dear Mary Ann,
>
> How are you? I'm having a great time in Los Angeles! Right now, I'm eating lunch at a Mexican restaurant and writing postcards. I want to buy stamps at the post office and visit the museum. The post office is about five blocks from the restaurant. It's next to the museum.
>
> See you soon!
> Rafael

> Mary Ann Rogers
> 17 West Street
> El Paso, TX 79910

1. Where is Rafael? _He's in Los Angeles._

2. What is he doing now? _____

3. Who is Rafael writing a postcard to? _____

4. Where's the post office? _____

5. Where's the museum? _____

5 Read the letter. Answer the questions.

> Hi Susan,
>
> I love my new apartment. It's across from my children's school. There's also a grocery store next to it. My husband works there. He walks to work. There's an Italian restaurant on the corner of Maple Street and Pine Street. It's very good. I like it here, but I miss you. Please write.
>
> Your friend,
> Lin

1. Where is Lin's apartment? _It's across from her children's school._

2. Where is the grocery store? _____

3. How does Lin's husband get to work? _____

4. Is the Italian restaurant good? _____

Check your answers. See page 132.

1 Write sentences.

1. the train station / Where's / ?
   Where's the train station?

2. on the corner of / The grocery store / Broadway and Main / is / .
   _____

3. the shopping mall / get to / How / I / do / ?
   _____

4. next to / the train station / It's / .
   _____

5. left / on / Maple Street / Turn / .
   _____

2 Complete the conversations. Use the sentences from Exercise 1.

1. **A** How do I get to the post office?
   B *Turn left on Maple Street.*

2. **A** Where's the grocery store?
   B _____

3. **A** _____
   B The train station is on Fifth Avenue.

4. **A** _____
   B Go straight two blocks. The shopping mall is on Grant Street.

5. **A** Where's the park?
   B _____

Check your answers. See page 132.

3 Add capital letters.

> Janet lives at 3725 *D̶*elta *S̶*treet. She goes to school at
> Madison Adult School. She walks down delta street for
> three blocks and turns right on skyline drive. She goes
> two blocks and turns left on national avenue. The school
> is at 3500 national avenue, next to Bandini Bakery.

4 Correct the sentences.

1. She lives at Main Street.
   She lives on Main Street.

2. There is a library in the restaurant and the bank.
   _____

3. Go straight Main Street.
   _____

4. It's next in the school.
   _____

5. Turn left Main Street.
   _____

6. The coffee shop is across the school.
   _____

5 Complete the paragraph.

Dr. Singh works at Mercy Hospital. Mercy Hospital is ___*between*___
                                                      1. between / on
a park and a shopping mall. He also teaches at Jefferson College. Jefferson

College is _____ from Jefferson Courthouse. He drives down Main
          2. across / between
Street for ten blocks and _____ left on Memorial Drive. He goes
                          3. cross / turns
five blocks and _____ right _____ Jefferson Avenue.
                4. goes to / turns   5. between / on
Jefferson College is at 2600 Jefferson Avenue, _____ Jefferson
                                               6. across / on the corner of
Avenue and Madison Street.

Check your answers. See page 133.

1 Look at the bold word. Cross out the word that is different.

1. **DMV**   license   ~~menu~~
2. **hospital**   doctor   teacher
3. **library**   books   gas
4. **playground**   children   museum
5. **post office** dictionaries   letters
6. **coffee shop** classrooms   restaurants

2 Complete the puzzle.

| bank | DMV | hospital | house | library | museum | park | school |

Down

1. Children play at the _____ .
3. The _____ has books.
5. The _____ has paintings.

Across

2. The teacher works at the _____ .
4. You get a driver's license at the _____ .
6. The _____ has money.
7. Dr. Ngyuen works at the _____ .
8. She lives in a _____ .

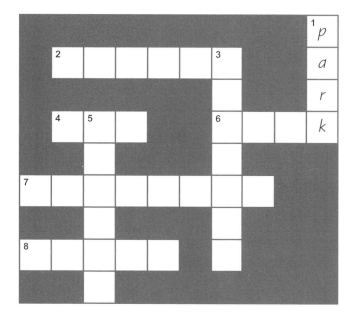

Check your answers. See page 133.

3 Look at the store directory. Circle the answers.

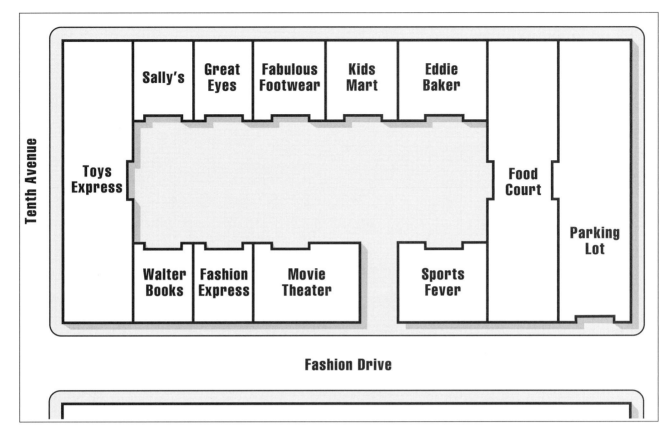

1. Where's Sports Fever?
   a. next to Fashion Express
   b. across from Great Eyes
   c. between Eddie Baker and the Food Court
   (d.) across from the movie theater

2. Where's Walter Books?
   a. across from Sally's
   b. next to Sally's
   c. between Sally's and Fashion Express
   d. near the Food Court

3. Where's the Food Court?
   a. on Tenth Avenue and Fashion Drive
   b. next to Great Eyes
   c. across from Kids Mart
   d. next to the parking lot

4. What's across from Great Eyes?
   a. Fashion Express
   b. Sports Fever
   c. Fabulous Footwear
   d. Eddie Baker

5. What's on the corner of Fashion Drive and Tenth Avenue?
   a. a parking lot
   b. the Food Court
   c. Toys Express
   d. Kids Mart

6. What's next to Great Eyes?
   a. Fashion Express
   b. Sally's
   c. Walter Books
   d. Tenth Avenue

Check your answers. See page 133.

Lesson A *Get ready*

1 Match the words.

1. take   *c*   a. home
2. read   ____   b. for work
3. leave ____   c. a break
4. catch ____   d. the bus
5. buy   ____   e. a schedule
6. get   ____   f. a snack

2 Look at the pictures. Write the words from Exercise 1.

take a break _____

_____

_____

_____

_____

_____

Check your answers. See page 133.

3 Match the times with the words.

1. 1:05   _f_   a. eight-forty-five
2. 2:45   ____   b. eleven-fifteen
3. 3:20   ____   c. five-fifteen
4. 4:50   ____   d. four-fifty
5. 5:15   ____   e. nine o'clock
6. 7:30   ____   f. one-oh-five
7. 8:45   ____   g. seven-thirty
8. 9:00   ____   h. ten o'clock
9. 10:00   ____   i. three-twenty
10. 11:15   ____   j. two-forty-five

4 Look at the clocks. Write the times in numbers.

1. ___12:00___
2. _____
3. _____
4. _____

5. _____
6. _____
7. _____
8. _____

5 Look at the clocks. Write the times in words.

1. ___six-ten___
2. _____
3. _____
4. _____

5. _____
6. _____
7. _____
8. _____

Check your answers. See page 133.

What do you do in the evening?

Study the chart on page 123.

1 Complete the sentences.

1. **A** What _____*do*_____ you do on Friday evening?
   (do / does)

   B I _____*go*_____ to the library and I _____ .
   (go / goes)   (study / studies)

2. **A** What _____ your brother do on Friday evening?
   (do / does)

   B He _____ soccer.
   (play / plays)

3. **A** What does your husband do on Saturday morning?

   B He _____ shopping.
   (go / goes)

4. **A** What _____ your sister do on Saturday night?
   (do / does)

   B She _____ TV.
   (watch / watches)

5. **A** What do your sons do on Sunday?

   B They _____ and they _____ .
   (read / reads)   (exercise / exercises)

2 Write a conversation. Use the sentences in the box.

Speaker A	Speaker B
What do you do at night?	It's at the Washington Community School.
Where's your class?	I usually go to class.
Do you study English?	Yes, I do.

1. **A** *What do you do at night?* _____

2. **B** _____

3. **A** _____

4. **B** _____

5. **A** _____

6. **B** _____

Check your answers. See page 133.

3 Complete the sentences.

1. **A** What do you do in the afternoon?

   B I _____*study*_____ English.

2. **A** What does she do in the evening?

   B She _____ TV.

3. **A** What does he do in the morning?

   B He _____ .

4. **A** What do you do on Saturday night?

   B I _____ to music.

5. **A** What do they do on Sunday afternoon?

   B They _____ in the garden.

4 Write questions.

1. morning   **A** *What do you do in the morning?* _____

   B I play soccer.

2. evening   **A** _____

   B I pay bills.

3. afternoon **A** _____

   B I go shopping.

4. Saturday   **A** _____

   B I go to the park.

Check your answers. See page 133.

I go to work at 8:00.

1 Complete the chart.

eight-thirty	June	night
eleven	Monday	Thursday afternoon
the evening	the morning	Wednesday night

at	in	on
eight-thirty		

2 Read Christina's calendar. Complete the sentences. Use *at*, *in*, or *on*.

Christina's Calendar

Sunday	Monday	Tuesday	Wednesday	Thursday	Friday	Saturday
	1 10:00 a.m. English class	**2** 9:00 a.m. volunteer	**3** 10:00 a.m. English class	**4** 1:00 p.m. work	**5** 10:00 a.m. English class	**6** 11 a.m. work
7 7:00 p.m. Malik's birthday party!	**8** 10:00 a.m. English class	**9** 7:30 p.m. PTA meeting	**10** 10:00 a.m. English class	**11** 1:00 p.m. work	**12** 10:00 a.m. English class	**13** 11 a.m. work

1. *A* What time does Christina
   volunteer on Tuesday the 2nd?
   B She volunteers ___at___ 9:00 a.m.

2. *A* When is Malik's birthday party?
   B It's _____ 7:00 p.m. _____
   Sunday.

3. *A* When does the PTA meeting start?
   B It starts _____ 7:30 _____ the
   evening _____ Tuesday the 9th.

4. *A* When is work?
   B It starts _____ 1:00 p.m. _____
   Thursdays and _____ 11:00 a.m.
   _____ Saturdays.

Check your answers. See page 133.

3 Look at the bulletin board. Answer the questions.

1. What time is the Library Volunteers' meeting?

   The meeting is at 5:30 p.m.

2. What day is the school open house?

   _____

3. What time does the driving class start?

   _____

4. What time does the exercise class end?

   _____

5. What day is the job fair?

   _____

6. When does the job fair start?

   _____

7. What time does baseball practice end?

   _____

8. What date is the school open house?

   _____

Check your answers. See page 133.

1 Read the story. Circle the answers.

A Day at the Restaurant

Ibrahim works at a restaurant. He is a cook. The restaurant is open Tuesday to Sunday for lunch and dinner. He works very hard. He leaves for work early in the morning. He checks the food and writes the day's menu. At 11:00, he starts cooking lunch. He takes a break at 3:00. At 4:00, he gets ready to cook dinner. After dinner, he gets ready for the next day. He doesn't go home until late at night. He's always tired, but he's happy!

1. What does Ibrahim do early in the morning?
   a. He cooks.
   b. He goes home.
   c. He leaves for work.
   d. He takes a break.

2. What does Ibrahim do at 11:00?
   a. He starts cooking lunch.
   b. He goes home.
   c. He leaves for work.
   d. He writes the menu.

3. What does Ibrahim do at 3:00?
   a. He cooks.
   b. He leaves for work.
   c. He gets ready to cook dinner.
   d. He takes a break.

4. What does Ibrahim do late at night?
   a. He goes home.
   b. He leaves for work.
   c. He starts cooking.
   d. He takes a break.

2 Answer the questions. Use the story in Exercise 1.

1. Where does Ibrahim work?

   He works at a restaurant.

2. When does he leave for work?

   _____

3. What does he do at 4:00?

   _____

4. When does he go home?

   _____

Check your answers. See page 133.

3 Complete the chart.

a break	dinner	a shower
breakfast	lunch	to bed
the children to school	shopping	to work

eat	go	take
breakfast		

4 Complete the sentences. Use the words from Exercise 3.

1. **A** When do they _eat lunch_____ ?

   B _They eat lunch at 12 o'clock._____

2. **A** When do they _____ ?

   B _____

3. **A** When does he _____ ?

   B _____

4. **A** When does she _____ ?

   B _____

Check your answers. See page 134.

1 Write questions.

1. volunteer / does / When / she / ?

   When does she volunteer?

2. to work / she / go / does / What time / ?

   _____

3. on the weekend / do / What / you / do / ?

   _____

4. to the park / go / he / on Saturday morning / Does / ?

   _____

5. go to bed / your / What time / children / do / ?

   _____

6. does / the dog / walk / he / When / ?

   _____

2 Complete the conversations. Use the questions from Exercise 1.

1. **A** *When does she volunteer?*

   B She volunteers in the evening.

2. **A** _____

   B He walks the dog in the evening.

3. **A** _____

   B I work at a shopping mall on the weekend.

4. **A** _____

   B They go to bed at 9:00 p.m.

5. **A** _____

   B She goes to work at 8:00 a.m.

6. **A** _____

   B Yes, he does.

Check your answers. See page 134.

3 Add capital letters. Then rewrite the sentences.

1. ~~s~~usie works at the library, and she goes to school.
   S

2. she works on monday, wednesday, and friday.

3. she begins work at 9:00 a.m.

4. she has lunch from 12:00 to 1:00 p.m.

5. she finishes work at 5:00 p.m.

6. on tuesday and thursday, she doesn't work. she goes to school.

_____Susie works at the library, and she goes to school._____

_____

_____

_____

_____

_____

_____

4 Complete the e-mail. Use *at*, *in*, or *on*.

○ ○ ○   Inbox (New Message)

Inbox
Outbox
Trash

hamidq@cup.org
Re: Daily Schedule

My daily schedule isn't hard. ___On___ Monday, I usually get up
                                   1.
_____ 7:00 _____ the morning. _____ 8:00, I leave for
    2.   3.   4.
work. I eat lunch _____ the afternoon because I am so busy. I
                      5.
leave for home _____ 6:00 _____ the evening. This is my
                   6.   7.
schedule Tuesday to Friday, too. _____ Saturday, I go to my
                                     8.
friend's house. _____ Sunday morning, I do something with my
                    9.
wife and children.

Check your answers. See page 134.

Time **71**

1 Write the day for each abbreviation.

1. Sun. _____Sunday_____
2. Mon. _____
3. Tues. _____
4. Wed. _____
5. Thurs. _____
6. Fri. _____
7. Sat. _____

Sun.	Mon.	Tues.	Wed.	Thurs.	Fri.	Sat.
1	2	3	4	5	6	7
8	9	10	11	12	13	14

2 Write the month for each abbreviation.

1. Jan. _____January_____
2. Feb. _____
3. Mar. _____
4. Apr. _____
5. Aug. _____
6. Sept. _____
7. Oct. _____
8. Nov. _____
9. Dec. _____

Jan.	Feb.	Mar.
Apr.	May	June
July	Aug.	Sept.
Oct.	Nov.	Dec.

3 Look at the bold word. Cross out the word that is different.

1. **read**	a book	~~a movie~~	a newspaper
2. **watch**	a movie	TV	the radio
3. **listen to**	music	a newspaper	the radio
4. **go to**	work	the park	homework
5. **cook**	bed	breakfast	lunch
6. **finish**	work	the park	homework
7. **drink**	English	coffee	water
8. **play**	baseball	TV	soccer
9. **study**	January	English	writing
10. **take**	a class	a soccer game	the bus

Check your answers. See page 134.

4 Look at the class schedule. Circle the answers.

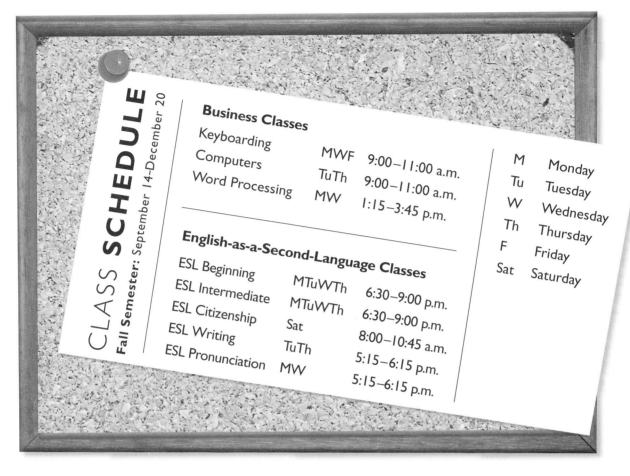

CLASS SCHEDULE
Fall Semester: September 14–December 20

Business Classes

Keyboarding	MWF	9:00–11:00 a.m.
Computers	TuTh	9:00–11:00 a.m.
Word Processing	MW	1:15–3:45 p.m.

English-as-a-Second-Language Classes

ESL Beginning	MTuWTh	6:30–9:00 p.m.
ESL Intermediate	MTuWTh	6:30–9:00 p.m.
ESL Citizenship	Sat	8:00–10:45 a.m.
ESL Writing	TuTh	5:15–6:15 p.m.
ESL Pronunciation	MW	5:15–6:15 p.m.

M	Monday
Tu	Tuesday
W	Wednesday
Th	Thursday
F	Friday
Sat	Saturday

1. What semester is this schedule for?
   a. Fall
   b. Summer
   c. Spring
   d. Winter

2. When does the semester begin?
   a. September 14
   b. September 20
   c. December 14
   d. December 20

3. When does the semester end?
   a. September 14
   b. September 20
   c. December 14
   d. December 20

4. What class meets on Saturday?
   a. Computers
   b. ESL Citizenship
   c. ESL Writing
   d. ESL Pronunciation

5. When are the computer classes?
   a. Monday, Wednesday, and Friday
   b. Monday and Wednesday
   c. Tuesday and Thursday
   d. Saturday

6. When are the Beginning ESL classes?
   a. in the morning
   b. on the weekend
   c. in the afternoon
   d. in the evening

Check your answers. See page 134.

Shopping

1 Complete the words.

1. ap _p_ l _e_ s
2. b ____ n ____ n ____ s
3. bre ____ ____
4. ch ____ e ____ e
5. c ____ ____ kies
6. ____ i ____ k
7. on ____ o ____ s
8. ____ ota ____ oes
9. to ____ at ____ es

2 Look at the pictures. Write the words from Exercise 1.

Everyday Low Prices!

This week only! Holiday Specials! 4th of July Blowout

SaveMore Supermarket
the place to shop for all your party needs

$2.49

$2.29

$2.99

1. _____milk_____

2. _____

3. _____

$4.00

$2.50

99¢

4. _____

5. _____

6. _____

$1.90

$1.79

$2.69

7. _____

8. _____

9. _____

Check your answers. See page 134.

3 List the items in Exercise 2 from the lowest price (99¢) to the highest price ($4.00).

1. _bananas 99¢_   4. _____   7. _____

2. _____   5. _____   8. _____

3. _____   6. _____   9. _cheese $4.00_

4 Match the words with the numbers.

1. five dollars and fifty-nine cents   _d_   a. $3.19

2. three dollars and ninety-nine cents ____   b. $16.09

3. nine dollars and eleven cents ____   c. $4.69

4. twenty dollars and twenty-five cents ____   d. $5.59

5. twelve dollars and thirty-five cents ____   e. $9.11

6. four dollars and sixty-nine cents ____   f. $10.49

7. three dollars and nineteen cents ____   g. $12.35

8. sixteen dollars and nine cents ____   h. $3.99

9. ten dollars and forty-nine cents ____   i. $60.09

10. sixty dollars and nine cents ____   j. $20.25

5 Read the prices. Write the numbers.

1. nine dollars and fifty-nine cents   _$9.59_

2. two dollars and twenty-five cents   _____

3. eight dollars and thirty cents   _____

4. five dollars and ten cents   _____

5. six dollars and forty-one cents   _____

6. fifteen dollars and ninety-nine cents   _____

7. ten dollars and sixty-two cents   _____

8. twenty dollars and fifteen cents   _____

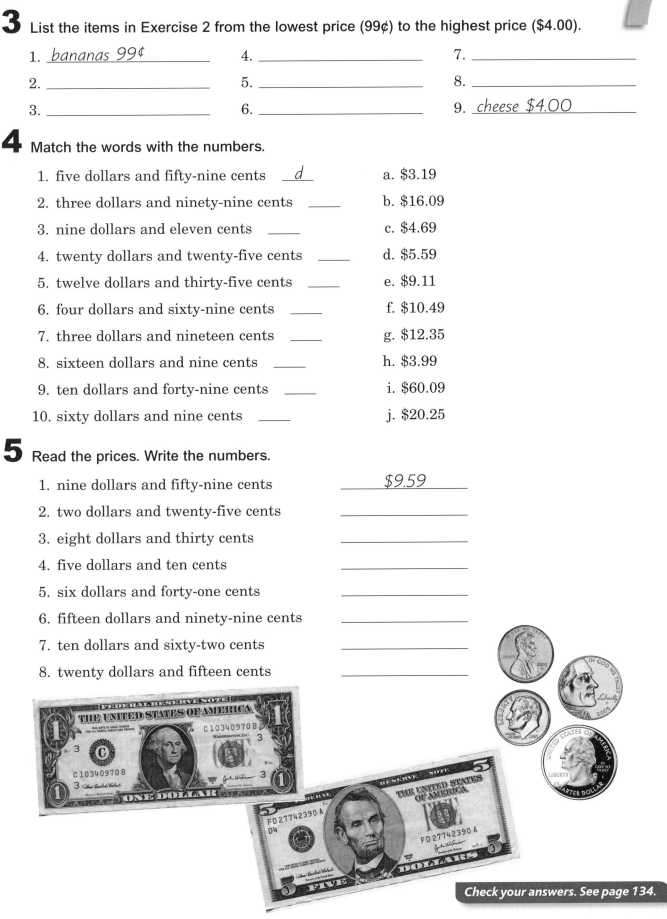

Check your answers. See page 134.

How many? How much?

1 Complete the chart.

apples	cheese	eggs	milk	peaches	rice	sugar
bananas	coffee	juice	oranges	pies	strawberries	water

How many . . . ?	How much . . . ?
apples	cheese

2 Write questions. Use *How many* or *How much*.

1. **A** *How many apples do you need?* _____

   B I need a lot of apples.

2. **A** _____

   B She needs a lot of sugar.

3. **A** _____

   B They need a lot of strawberries.

4. **A** _____

   B You need a lot of eggs.

5. **A** _____

   B He needs a lot of water.

6. **A** _____

   B I need a lot of oranges.

Check your answers. See page 134.

3 Write a conversation. Use the sentences in the box.

Speaker A	Speaker B
We need five or six.	OK. How many apples?
Not much.	OK. See you later.
We apples and juice.	To the grocery store.
Where are you going?	How much juice do we need?

1. **A** _Where are you going?_ _____
2. **B** _____
3. **A** _____
4. **B** _____
5. **A** _____
6. **B** _____
7. **A** _____
8. **B** _____

4 Complete the sentences.

a lot	many	need
does	much	needs

1. How ____much____ milk does he need?
2. We _____ a lot of meat.
3. How many peaches _____ she need?
4. He doesn't need _____ bananas.
5. She _____ five eggs.
6. I need _____ of apples.

Check your answers. See page 135.

Are there any bananas?

1 Look at the picture. Answer the questions.

1. **A** Are there any bananas?

   B *Yes, there are.*

2. **A** Is there any coffee?

   B *No, there isn't.*

3. **A** Are there any blueberries?

   B _____

4. **A** Is there any bread?

   B _____

5. **A** Are there any pies?

   B _____

6. **A** Is there a pineapple?

   B _____

7. **A** Is there any soda?

   B _____

8. **A** Is there any tea?

   B _____

9. **A** Is there any apple juice?

   B _____

10. **A** Is there any water?

   B _____

2 Unscramble the letters. Write the food containers.

1. two ____*bags*____ of rice
   (agsb)

2. a _____ of orange juice
   (tlbeto)

3. six _____ of soda
   (sacn)

4. a _____ of tea
   (obx)

5. a _____ of water
   (gslsa)

6. two _____ of milk
   (toncars)

7. a _____ of bread
   (fola)

8. a _____ of cookies
   (pagecka)

Check your answers. See page 135.

3 Complete the charts. Write the singular form.

Singular	Plural		Singular	Plural
1. *box*	boxes		4.	packages
2.	cartons		5.	cans
3.	bottles		6.	bags

4 Read the sign. Circle the answers.

SAM'S BREAK STAND

COFFEE $1.25/CUP	TEA $.75/CUP
SODA $.75/CAN	WATER $1.05/BOTTLE
MILK $1.00/CARTON	JUICE $.70/BOX

1. How much is one cup of coffee?
   a. 70¢
   b. 75¢
   c. $1.00
   (d.) $1.25

2. How much are a box of juice and a carton of milk?
   a. 75¢
   b. $1.25
   c. $1.50
   d. $1.70

3. How much is a cup of tea?
   a. sixty cents
   b. seventy cents
   c. seventy-five cents
   d. one dollar

4. How much is a bottle of water?
   a. seventy-five cents
   b. one dollar and five cents
   c. one-twenty-five
   d. one-fifty

5 Complete the sentences. Use *There is* or *There are*.

1. _____*There are*_____ three boxes of tea.
2. _____ a carton of milk.
3. _____ a bottle of water.
4. _____ six bottles of juice.
5. _____ two packages of meat.
6. _____ twelve cans of soda.
7. _____ one bag of flour.
8. _____ a dozen eggs

Check your answers. See page 135.

Lesson D Reading

1 Find the words.

ATM	card	credit	dollar	nickel	quarter
bill	check	dime	half	penny	

```
q  u  a  r  t  e  r  i  c
e  e  t  d  i  m  e  i  a
n  i  m  o  n  m  t  c  h
l  h  c  l  i  c  e  i  a
a  t  h  l  c  a  h  c  l
b  d  e  a  k  r  b  a  f
k  t  c  r  e  d  i  t  i
y  c  k  l  l  f  l  n  e
p  e  n  n  y  r  l  c  n
```

2 Complete the questions.

dime	five	one	quarter	ten	twenty

1. **A** Do you have change for a _____*quarter*_____ ?

   B Sure. Here are five nickels.

2. **A** Do you have change for a _____ -dollar bill?

   B Sure. Here are four quarters.

3. **A** Do you have change for a _____ -dollar bill?

   B Sure. Here are 2 ten-dollar bills.

4. **A** Do you have change for a _____ ?

   B Sure. Here are two nickels.

5. **A** Do you have change for a _____ -dollar bill?

   B Sure. Here are 5 one-dollar bills.

6. **A** Do you have change for a _____ -dollar bill?

   B Sure. Here are 2 five-dollar bills.

Check your answers. See page 135.

3 Complete the sentences.

bread	grocery	milk	onions	rice	tea

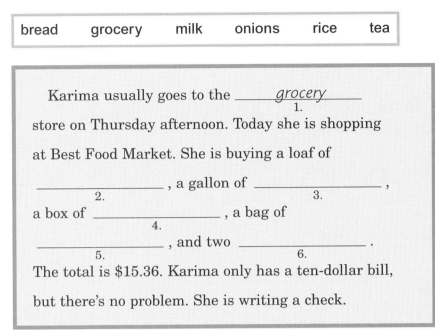

    Karima usually goes to the _____*grocery*_____
1.
store on Thursday afternoon. Today she is shopping
at Best Food Market. She is buying a loaf of

_____ , a gallon of _____ ,
      2.   3.
a box of _____ , a bag of
                   4.

_____ , and two _____ .
      5.   6.
The total is $15.36. Karima only has a ten-dollar bill,

but there's no problem. She is writing a check.

4 Answer the questions about Karima. Use the information from Exercise 3.

1. What does Karima usually do on Thursday afternoon?

   *She usually goes to the grocery store.*_____

2. Where is she shopping today?

_____

3. How much milk is she buying?

_____

4. How much rice is she buying?

_____

5. How many onions is she buying?

_____

6. How much is the total?

_____

7. How much money does she have?

_____

8. What is she writing?

_____

Check your answers. See page 135.

1 Write questions.

1. we / Do / of milk / need / a carton / ?

   Do we need a carton of milk?

2. the refrigerator / juice / there / any / Is / in / ?

   _____

3. she / a bottle / Is / buying / of water / ?

   _____

4. on the shelf / Are / any / there / bananas / ?

   _____

5. How much / do / you / coffee / need / ?

   _____

6. there / oranges / How many / are / on the table / ?

   _____

7. have / she / How much / does / in her purse / money / ?

   _____

8. favorite grocery store / is / What / his / ?

   _____

2 Complete the sentences.

bag	box	carton	credit card	loaf	three

James,

Please buy some groceries. We need a _____carton_____
1.
of milk, _____ onions, a _____ of
2.   3.
tea, a _____ of rice, and a _____ of
4.   5.
bread. When you pay, use the _____ .
6.

Thanks,
Meg

Check your answers. See page 135.

3 Look at the picture. Complete the sentences.

1. Julie is buying a _____package_____ of cookies.
2. She is buying a _____ of coffee.
3. She is buying a _____ of onions.
4. She is buying a _____ of milk.
5. She is buying a _____ of meat.
6. She is buying a _____ of tea.
7. She is buying _____ tomatoes.
8. She is buying _____ pineapple.

4 Add capital letters and commas.

$\overset{W}{\text{w}}$alter is a regular customer at Happy Day Supermarket. he usually goes three times a week. everybody knows him. today he's buying three apples two oranges a package of cookies and a can of soda. he needs to pay $8.95. walter only has a five-dollar bill a one-dollar bill and a quarter. he can write a check.

5 Rewrite the paragraph in Exercise 4. Change *Walter* to *I*.

I am a regular customer at Happy Day Supermarket.

_____

_____

_____

_____

_____

_____

_____

Check your answers. See page 135.

1 Look at the check. Answer the questions.

WALTER TAYLOR   1702
4217 LINDEN AVENUE
DAYTON, OH 45432
                                            DATE *July 3, 2008*

PAY TO THE
ORDER OF   *Happy Day Supermarket* $ *8.95*

Eight and 95/100 ~~~~~~~~~~~~~~~~~~~~~~~~~~~~~~ DOLLARS   Security Features Included. Details on Back.

Dayton Bank

Dayton Bank, FA
2210 Jersey Blvd.
Dayton, OH 45449

MEMO *groceries*   *Walter Taylor*   MP

⑆000000000⑆   000000000⑆' 0000

1. What's the date? *July 3, 2008*

2. Who's the check to? _____

3. Who's the check from? _____

4. How much money is the check for? _____

5. What's the name of the bank? _____

6. What's the check number? _____

2 Complete the check for $42.68. Write the amount in both numbers and words.
Write the date. Sign your name.

                                                                628

                                            DATE _____

PAY TO THE
ORDER OF   *Acme Grocery* $ _____

_____ DOLLARS   Security Features Included. Details on Back.

Dayton Bank

Dayton Bank, FA
2210 Jersey Blvd.
Dayton, OH 45449

MEMO _____   _____   MP

⑆000000000⑆   000000000⑆' 0000

Check your answers. See page 135.

3 Complete the puzzle.

are	bill	card	check	half	many	nickel
banana	bottle	change	groceries	is	much	

Across

1. How _____ juice do we need?

3. There are two quarters in a _____-dollar.

7. She buys _____ every week.

8. _____ there any cookies on the shelf?

9. Walter is writing a _____ at the supermarket.

10. How _____ oranges do we need?

11. I need a _____ of orange juice.

12. I have a credit _____ .

Down

2. Do you have _____ for a dollar?

4. There are five pennies in a _____ .

5. _____ there any more coffee?

6. A _____ is yellow.

11. She has only a five-dollar _____ .

Check your answers. See page 136.

1 Unscramble the letters. Write the words.

1. yobusb _____*busboy*_____   5. aitressw _____

2. koco _____   6. torcod _____

3. senur _____   7. sngiunr natsissta _____

4. eraiwt _____   8. shcaier _____

2 Where do people work? Use the words from Exercise 1.

1. restaurant _____*busboy*_____ _____ _____

_____ _____

2. hospital _____ _____ _____

3 Match the occupations with the tools and equipment.

a

e

1. busboy
2. cashier
3. construction worker
4. cook
5. doctor
6. electrician
7. office worker
8. truck driver

b

f

c

g

d

h

Check your answers. See page 136.

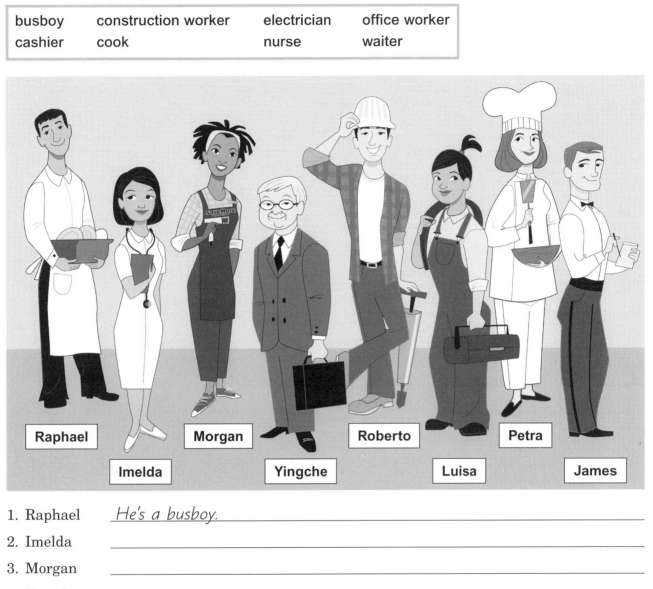

4 Look at the picture. Write sentences. Use *He's* and *She's* and the words in the box.

busboy	construction worker	electrician	office worker
cashier	cook	nurse	waiter

1. Raphael *He's a busboy.*
2. Imelda _____
3. Morgan _____
4. Yingche _____
5. Roberto _____
6. Luisa _____
7. Petra _____
8. James _____

Check your answers. See page 136.

I was a teacher.

Study the chart on page 124.

1 Complete the sentences. Use *am*, *are*, *is*, *was*, or *were*.

Before	Now
1. She ____was____ a nurse.	She ____is____ a student.
2. He _____ an office worker.	He _____ a manager.
3. They _____ electricians.	They _____ construction workers.
4. I _____ a teacher.	I _____ a student.
5. She _____ a student.	She _____ a housekeeper.
6. They _____ waiters.	They _____ cashiers.
7. He _____ a nursing assistant.	He _____ a doctor.
8. He _____ a truck driver.	He _____ a cook.

2 Complete the conversations. Use the correct form of *be*.

1. **A** What does Gregory do?

   B He works in a hospital.
   He _____is_____ a nurse.

   A Really? _____ he a nurse
   before in his country?

   B Yes, he _____ .

2. **A** Where does Anita work?

   B She works in a bank.
   She _____ a manager.

   A Really? _____ she a manager
   before in her country?

   B No, she _____ .
   She _____ a teacher.

Check your answers. See page 136.

3 Write questions.

1. waiters

   A *Were they waiters before?*

   B No, they weren't. They were office workers.

2. teacher

   A _____

   B No, she wasn't. She was a nurse.

3. electricians

   A _____

   B No, they weren't. They were construction workers.

4. manager

   A _____

   B No, she wasn't. She was a teacher.

5. nurse

   A _____

   B No, he wasn't. He was a doctor.

4 Answer the questions. Use *No.*

1. manager

   A Was he a cashier before?

   B *No, he wasn't. He was a manager.*

2. waiter

   A Was he a busboy before?

   B _____

3. nurse

   A Were you a doctor before?

   B _____

4. waitress

   A Was she a housewife before?

   B _____

5. students

   A Were they teachers before?

   B _____

Check your answers. See page 136.

Can you cook?

Study the chart on page 126.

1 Look at the chart. Answer the questions.

	Drive a truck	Work with a computer	Paint	Fix a car	Speak Spanish
Mary				✓	✓
Daniel	✓		✓	✓	
Vera		✓			✓
Brenda	✓	✓			

1. Can Daniel drive a truck?   *Yes, he can.*
2. Can Brenda speak Spanish?   _____
3. Can Brenda and Vera paint?   _____
4. Can Mary and Vera speak Spanish?   _____
5. Can Daniel work with a computer?   _____
6. Can Mary fix a car?   _____

2 Read the job ads. Match the names in Exercise 1 with the jobs.

1

Office Worker Needed. Can you work with a computer? Speak Spanish? Then call today! 555-7797

2

Part-Time Driver Needed. Can you drive a truck? Can you work with a computer? Must have office experience, too. Call Mondays. 555-3606

3

Painter Needed. Can you paint? Drive a truck? We can train you on the job. Call now! 555-1234

4

Auto Mechanic Needed. Can you fix a car? Speak Spanish? Call us! 555-0602

_____*Vera*_____   _____   _____   _____

Check your answers. See page 136.

3 Look at the picture. Write questions and answers.

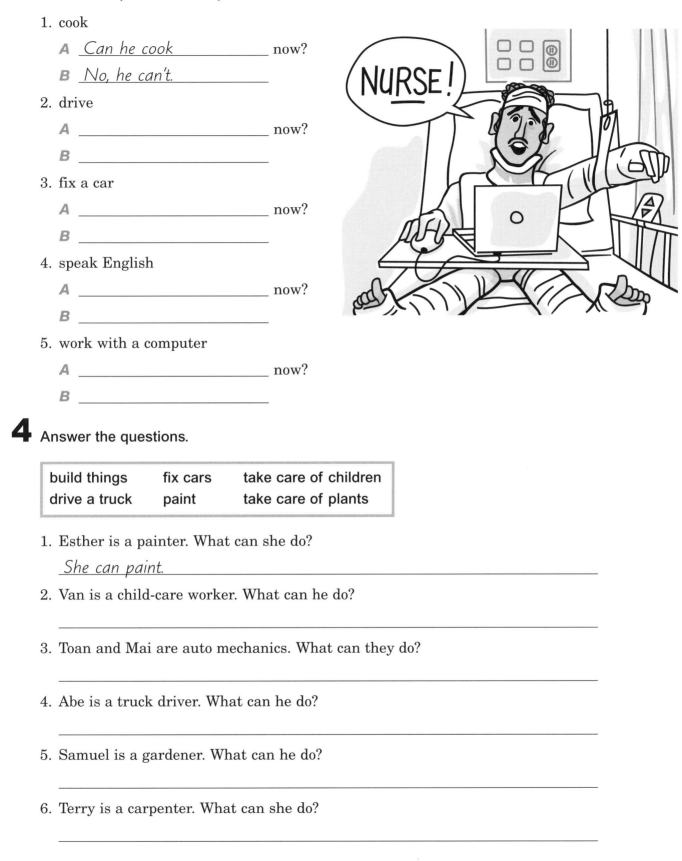

1. cook

   A _Can he cook_____ now?

   B _No, he can't._____

2. drive

   A _____ now?

   B _____

3. fix a car

   A _____ now?

   B _____

4. speak English

   A _____ now?

   B _____

5. work with a computer

   A _____ now?

   B _____

4 Answer the questions.

build things	fix cars	take care of children
drive a truck	paint	take care of plants

1. Esther is a painter. What can she do?

   _She can paint._____

2. Van is a child-care worker. What can he do?

   _____

3. Toan and Mai are auto mechanics. What can they do?

   _____

4. Abe is a truck driver. What can he do?

   _____

5. Samuel is a gardener. What can he do?

   _____

6. Terry is a carpenter. What can she do?

   _____

Check your answers. See page 136.

1 Find the words.

drugstore	hospital	restaurant
factory	hotel	school
home	office	store

```
f  r  c  e  a  a  l  y  r  o
a  e  o  h  o  p  s  c  l  d
t  s  u  o  h  o  t  e  l  r
o  t  r  s  c  h  o  o  l  u
f  a  t  p  l  o  r  f  s  g
f  u  r  i  f  m  e  f  h  s
a  r  o  t  e  e  r  i  r  t
c  a  o  a  m  o  c  r  o
h  n  m  l  t  h  u  e  m  r
o  t (f  a  c  t  o  r  y) e
o  h  o  p  r  e  h  o  m  l
```

2 Complete the sentences. Use the words from Exercise 1.

1. A housekeeper works in a _____ *hotel* _____ .

2. A pharmacist works in a _____ .

3. A nurse works in a _____ .

4. A housewife works at _____ .

5. A waitress works in a _____ .

6. A salesperson works in a _____ .

7. A factory worker works in a _____ .

8. An office worker works in an _____ .

9. A teacher works in a _____ .

Check your answers. See page 136.

3 Write a conversation. Use the sentences in the box.

Speaker A	Speaker B
Hi, Francisco. What job are you looking for?	My name is Francisco.
OK. What can you do?	I'm looking for a job as a salesperson.
Hello. What's your name?	I can sell things. I can talk to customers.

1. **A** _Hello. What's your name?_
2. **B** _____
3. **A** _____
4. **B** _____
5. **A** _____
6. **B** _____

4 Read the story. Answer the questions.

> Francisco is looking for a job as a salesperson. He was a salesperson in his country. Now he's a busboy. He wants to find a job as a salesperson in this country. Francisco has many skills. He can sell things in a store. He can talk to customers. He can speak several languages.

1. Is Francisco looking for a job?

   Yes, he is.

2. What was Francisco's job in his country?

   _____

3. What is Francisco's job now?

   _____

4. What job does Francisco want?

   _____

5. What are Francisco's skills?

   _____

6. Can he speak more than one language?

   _____

Check your answers. See page 136.

1 Make questions.

1. work with / a computer / she / Can / ?

   Can she work with a computer?

2. a nurse / country / she / her / Was / in / ?

   _____

3. his / Was / in / a waiter / he / country / ?

   _____

4. a car / he / fix / Can / ?

   _____

5. looking for / a job / Ana / Is / ?

   _____

6. skills / are / your / What / ?

   _____

2 Complete the conversations. Use *can*, *can't*, *is*, or *was*.

1. **A** __Can__ she work with computers?

   B Yes, she _____ .

2. **A** _____ he a waiter now?

   B No, he _____ a waiter in his country.

3. **A** _____ they type and write reports?

   B No, they _____ .

4. **A** _____ she an office worker now?

   B Yes, she _____ .

5. **A** _____ he use a cash register?

   B No, he _____ .

6. **A** _____ she a nurse before?

   B Yes, she _____ .

3 Correct the sentences.

> work
> I wrok at the Market Street Deli. It is a
>   1.
> small retsaraunt in Dallas. I am a waitre .
>   2.   3.
> I was a bsuboy . I can coko , too. I want to
>   4.   5.
> be a mangaer .
>   6.

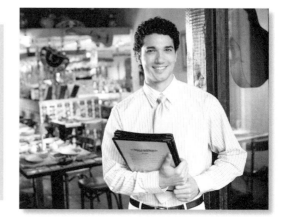

Check your answers. See page 137.

4 Correct the sentences. Then rewrite them.

1. Five years ago, Ana ~~is~~ *was* a manager in her country.

   Five years ago, Ana was a manager in her country.

2. Now she was a cashier.

   _____

3. She can using a cash register.

   _____

4. She can count money and talks to customers.

   _____

5. Ana and her husband is happy with their jobs in this country.

   _____

6. Before they are managers. Now they having new jobs.

   _____

5 Read the paragraph. Then rewrite it. Use *was*, *were*, *wasn't*, or *weren't*.

> ## Tonight at Pizza Palace
>
> Jim is at Pizza Palace tonight. His boss is there, too. Jim is very busy. There are many customers in the restaurant. They aren't happy because their food isn't ready. The customers are angry. They are very hungry. Jim is hungry, too. He's also tired. Jim is ready to go home!

Last Saturday at Pizza Palace

Jim was at Pizza Palace last Saturday.

_____

_____

_____

_____

_____

Check your answers. See page 137.

Another view

1 Look at the bold word. Cross out the word that is different.

1. **custodian**	office building	school	~~beauty salon~~
2. **waitress**	salesperson	restaurant	busboy
3. **office worker**	type	answer the phone	give change
4. **cashier**	count money	serve food	give change
5. **busboy**	cars	dishes	tables
6. **nursing assistant**	write reports	fix a car	help elderly people
7. **salesperson**	store	shop	restaurant
8. **hairstylist**	cut	cook	wash
9. **housekeeper**	paint rooms	clean rooms	make beds
10. **doctor**	hospital	shopping mall	medical office

2 Complete the chart.

Skill

clean rooms	sell things
cut hair	take care of children
serve food	work with computers

Place of work

beauty salon	office
day-care center	restaurant
hotel	store

Occupation	Skill	Place of work
1. child-care worker	*take care of children*	*day-care center*
2. hairstylist		
3. housekeeper		
4. office worker		
5. salesperson		
6. waiter		

Check your answers. See page 137.

3 Read each sentence. Write two more sentences. Use the words from Exercise 2.

	Place	Skill
1. Gina is a housekeeper.	_She works in a hotel._	_She cleans rooms._
2. Tim is a waiter.	_____	_____
3. Carol is a salesperson.	_____	_____
4. Tom is an office worker.	_____	_____
5. John is a hairstylist.	_____	_____
6. Al is a child-care worker.	_____	_____

4 Look at the job application. Answer the questions.

Employment Application

Name _Gloria Fuentes_	Soc. Sec. No. _000-99-5554_
Address _2733 Beech Street, Apt. 5 Miami, Florida 74354_	Phone _(305) 555-2306_
Are you 16 years or older? Yes ✓ No __	Position desired _nursing assistant_

Employment history (List most recent job first.)

Dates (from – to)	Employer name and address	Position
2006ñpresent	_Manor Inn Nursing Home 645 Palm Avenue, Miami, FL_	_certified nursing assistant_
_2004ñ2006_	_Family Fun Restaurant 3566 South 45th Street, Miami, FL_	_cashier_

Important: Show your Social Security card at the time you present this application.

1. Is Gloria working now? _Yes, she is._
2. What is Gloria's job? _____
3. Was she a nursing assistant before? _____
4. Where does she work? _____
5. Is she looking for a job? _____
6. When was she a cashier? _____

Check your answers. See page 137.

Daily living

1 Unscramble the letters. Write the words.

1. rion _____iron_____   6. ashtr _____

2. esshdi _____   7. uumcav _____

3. opm _____   8. shwa _____

4. swpee _____   9. pytme _____

5. eancl _____   10. tpain _____

2 Look at the picture. Write the words.

| empty | iron | paint | sweep | vacuum | wash |

1. _____paint_____

2. _____

3. _____

4. _____

5. _____

6. _____

Check your answers. See page 137.

3 Match the words.

1. clean _b_   a. the clothes

2. empty ____   b. the kitchen

3. iron ____   c. the bills

4. mop ____   d. the floor

5. paint ____   e. the rug

6. pay ____   f. the wall

7. vacuum ____   g. the trash

4 Complete the sentences.

1. He dried the _____*dishes*_____ .
   (dishes / floor)

2. She swept the _____ .
   (clothes / floor)

3. I painted the _____ .
   (garbage / house)

4. We vacuumed the _____ .
   (rug / clothes)

5. She paid the _____ .
   (bills / trash)

6. They washed the _____ .
   (clothes / vacuum)

7. He mopped the _____ .
   (rug / floor)

8. She emptied the _____ .
   (iron / trash)

5 Read the advertisement. Answer the questions.

1. How much is the vacuum cleaner?

   _$74.99_____

2. What is the company's name?

   _____

3. What is the company's phone number?

   _____

4. What city is the company in?

   _____

5. What state is the company in?

   _____

Super Vacuum Cleaner
X2R

The best vacuum cleaner ever!

Only $74⁹⁹!
Buy one today!
Sale until May 3rd!

AV

Acme Vacuums of Cincinnati, Ohio

(514) 555-8976

Check your answers. See page 137.

Study the chart on page 125.

1 Write the simple past of each verb.

1. clean   _____cleaned_____   6. iron   _____

2. cook   _____   7. mop   _____

3. dry   _____   8. paint   _____

4. dust   _____   9. vacuum   _____

5. empty   _____

2 Look at the pictures. Write the words from Exercise 1.

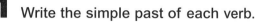

_____cleaned_____

_____

_____

_____

_____

_____

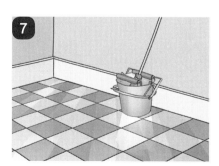

_____

_____

_____

Check your answers. See page 137.

3 Complete the conversations. Use the simple past, *did*, or *didn't*.

1. **A** __Did__ he wash the dishes?

   B No, he __didn't__ .

   He _____mopped_____ the floor.
   (mop)

2. **A** _____ he dust the furniture?

   B No, he _____ .

   He _____ the rug.
   (vacuum)

3. **A** _____ they cook the dinner?

   B Yes, they _____ .

   They also _____ the dishes.
   (dry)

4. **A** _____ she clean her bedroom?

   B No, she _____ .

   She _____ the kitchen.
   (clean)

5. **A** _____ she iron the clothes?

   B No, she _____ .

   She _____ the trash.
   (empty)

6. **A** _____ she dry the dishes?

   B No, she _____ .

   She _____ the dishes.
   (wash)

7. **A** _____ she mop the floor?

   B No, she _____ .

   She _____ the living room.
   (dust)

8. **A** _____ he clean his apartment?

   B No, he _____ .

   He _____ his family's house.
   (clean)

Check your answers. See page 137.

Lesson C *I paid the bills.*

Study the chart on page 125.

1 Look at the picture. Write the past tense of the verbs.

do	get	make	pay

Jin

2. _____ the laundry

Mei

1. ___*got*___ the mail

Jian

4. _____ lunch

Shufen

3. _____ the bills

2 Complete the sentences. Use the verbs from Exercise 1.

1. **A** Who ___*got*___ the mail?
   B *Mei did.* _____

2. **A** Who _____ lunch?
   B _____

3. **A** Who _____ the laundry?
   B _____

4. **A** Who _____ the bills?
   B _____

Check your answers. See page 138.

3 Look at the picture. Write the simple past of the verbs.

| buy | cut | make | sweep |

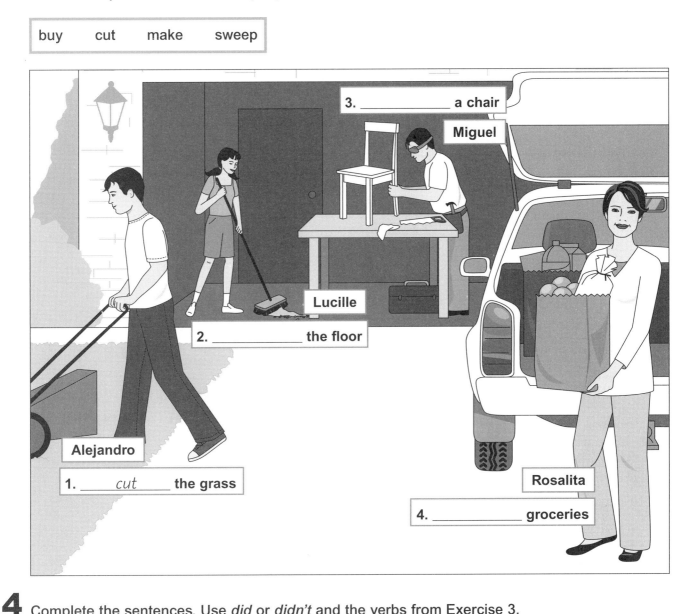

3. _____ a chair

Miguel

2. _____ the floor

Lucille

Alejandro

1. ___*cut*___ the grass

Rosalita

4. _____ groceries

4 Complete the sentences. Use *did* or *didn't* and the verbs from Exercise 3.

1. **A** Did Lucille buy groceries?

   B No, she ___*didn't*___ . She ___*swept*___ the floor.

2. **A** Did Alejandro make a chair?

   B No, he _____ . He _____ the grass.

3. **A** Did Miguel make a chair?

   B Yes, he _____ .

4. **A** Did Miguel buy groceries?

   B No, he _____ . He _____ a chair.

5. **A** Did Rosalita sweep the floor?

   B No, she _____ . She _____ groceries.

6. **A** Did Alejandro cut the grass?

   B Yes, he _____ .

Check your answers. See page 138.

Lesson D Reading

1 Find the words.

broom	iron	laundry	mower	stove
dustpan	kitchen	mail	sponge	vacuum

```
o  w  k  i  t  c  h  e  n  y
s  t  o  v  e  f  o  o  d  v
s  b  l  a  u  n  d  r  y  e
p  r  v  a  c  u  u  m  m  u
o  o  g  p  a  s  s  u  m  g
n  o  n  y  e  v  t  k  o  b
g  m  a  i  l  d  p  i  w  a
e  n  g  a  r  b  a  g  e  t
m  i  r  o  n  i  n  g  r  w
z  c  d  e  f  n  q  i  o  s
```

2 Complete the sentences. Use the past tense of the verb and the words from Exercise 1.

1. She _____*swept*_____ the floor with a _____*broom*_____ .
   (sweep)

2. He _____ soup on the _____ .
   (make)

3. She _____ the grass with the lawn _____ .
   (cut)

4. She _____ the dishes with a _____ .
   (wash)

5. They _____ the rug with a _____ cleaner.
   (clean)

6. Frank _____ the _____ from the mailbox.
   (get)

Check your answers. See page 138.

3 Read the story. Underline the people. Circle the chores.

Family Chores

The Cabrera family (cleaned their house) last Saturday. Mom swept the kitchen. Dad mopped the kitchen floor. He also cut the grass with the lawn mower. Dad and Yolanda washed the dishes. Roberto vacuumed the rugs in the living room. He and Sara made the beds. Sara emptied the trash and got the mail. After they finished the chores, they had dinner and watched a movie.

4 Who did each chore? Use the information from Exercise 3.

CABRERA FAMILY CHORES

	MOM	DAD	YOLANDA	ROBERTO	SARA
1. cut the grass		✓			
2. emptied the trash					
3. got the mail					
4. made the beds					
5. mopped the floor					
6. swept the kitchen					
7. washed the dishes					
8. vacuumed the rugs					

5 Answer the questions.

1. Did the Cabrera family clean their house on Sunday?

   No, they didn't. They cleaned it on Saturday.

2. Who cut the grass?

   _____

3. Who made the beds?

   _____

4. Who swept the kitchen?

   _____

5. Did Yolanda get the mail?

   _____

Check your answers. See page 138.

1 Read the chore chart. Answer the questions.

PERSON	CHORE	COMPLETED?
Jason	pay the bills	✓
Samantha	do the laundry	
Linda	vacuum the rug	✓
Jordan	make the beds	✓
John	sweep the kitchen	
Chantelle	make dinner	✓

1. Who paid the bills?

   Jason did.

2. Did Samantha do the laundry?

   _____

3. Who made the beds?

   _____

4. Did Chantelle make dinner?

   _____

5. Who vacuumed the rug?

   _____

6. Did John sweep the kitchen?

   _____

7. Did Jason vacuum the rug?

   _____

8. Did Jordan make dinner?

   _____

Check your answers. See page 138.

2 Complete the sentences.

bathroom	chores	grass	laundry	rug	weekend
bills	floor	groceries	mail	trash	works

Every _____weekend_____ , the Johnson family does _____ .
                1.   2.

Lucille buys _____ . Vince cuts the _____ . Lynn
                    3.   4.

cleans the _____ and sweeps the _____ . Nicky
                 5.   6.

gets the _____ and pays the _____ . Ida empties
               7.   8.

the _____ . Raymond does the _____ and
          9.   10.

vacuums the _____ . Everyone _____ very hard.
                   11.   12.

3 Rewrite the paragraph from Exercise 2. Use the simple past.

Last weekend, the Johnson family did chores.

_____

_____

_____

_____

_____

_____

_____

_____

_____

_____

_____

_____

_____

_____

_____

Check your answers. See page 138.

Another view

1 Look at the chart. Circle the answers.

Student	Check attendance	Help new students	Turn off lights and lock doors	Get class books	Help students with computer
Andrei	✓				
Soon-yi		✓			
Hector				✓	
Marjane			✓		
Salvatore					✓

RIVERVIEW **ADULT SCHOOL**: Tuesday's Classroom Duties

1. Who helped new students?
   a. Andrei
   b. Soon-yi
   c. Hector
   d. Salvatore

2. Who got the books?
   a. Andrei
   b. Hector
   c. Marjane
   d. Salvatore

3. Who locked the doors?
   a. Andrei
   b. Soon-yi
   c. Marjane
   d. Hector

4. Did Marjane turn off the lights?
   a. Yes, she did.
   b. No, she didn't.
   c. Marjane didn't.
   d. She checked attendance.

5. Did Andrei check attendance?
   a. Yes, I did.
   b. Yes, he did.
   c. No, he didn't.
   d. He turned off the lights.

6. Who helped students with the computer?
   a. Andrei
   b. Soon-yi
   c. Hector
   d. Salvatore

Check your answers. See page 138.

2 Complete the puzzle. Use the past tense.

Down

1. Sarah ____dusted____ the furniture.
(dust)

3. Grandma _____ some groceries.
(buy)

4. Mom _____ the bed.
(make)

5. Lei _____ her shirt.
(iron)

7. John _____ the trash.
(empty)

9. Jane _____ the grass.
(cut)

Across

2. Grandpa _____ the kitchen.
(sweep)

6. Ted _____ the rug.
(vacuum)

8. Charlie _____ the mail.
(get)

10. Mike _____ his house.
(paint)

11. Anne _____ the bills.
(pay)

Check your answers. See page 138.

Lesson A Get ready

1 Find the words.

| camping | canoeing | fishing | hiking | picnicking | play ball | swimming |

```
p  l  a  y  b  a  l  l  k
i  n  g  m  g  f  w  p  l
c  a  n  o  e  i  n  g  g
n  o  n  h  c  s  g  e (c)
i  c  i  a  k  h  b  k  a
c  a  n  i  i  i  y  f  m
k  h  i  k  i  n  g  i  p
i  o  f  e  i  g  g  n  i
n  i  l  a  g  g  k  i  n
g  s  w  i  m  m  i  n  g
```

2 Look at the picture. Use the words from Exercise 1.

1. _hiking_
2. _____
3. _____
4. _____
5. _____
6. _____
7. _____

Check your answers. See page 138.

3 Look at the chart. Circle the answers.

	🛶	⚽	🏊	⛺	🎣	🥾
Kent Park			✓	✓	✓	✓
Palisades Park	✓	✓		✓	✓	✓
Beaver Park		✓	✓			
Daniels Park			✓			✓
City Park	✓		✓		✓	

1. What parks have canoeing?
   a. Beaver Park and Daniels Park
   (b.) Palisades Park and City Park
   c. Daniels Park and Beaver Park
   d. Kent Park and Palisades Park

2. What park has swimming and soccer?
   a. Beaver Park
   b. Daniels Park
   c. Kent Park
   d. Palisades Park

3. What parks have fishing and hiking?
   a. Beaver Park and Palisades Park
   b. City Park and Kent Park
   c. Daniels Park and City Park
   d. Kent Park and Palisades Park

4. What parks have fishing and swimming?
   a. Beaver Park and City Park
   b. Kent Park and City Park
   c. Daniels Park and Kent Park
   d. Palisades Park and City Park

5. What park has canoeing and soccer?
   a. City Park
   b. Daniels Park
   c. Kent Park
   d. Palisades Park

6. What parks have camping?
   a. Beaver Park and City Park
   b. Daniels Park and Kent Park
   c. City Park and Palisades Park
   d. Kent Park and Palisades Park

Check your answers. See page 139.

What did you do yesterday?

Study the chart on page 125.

1 Complete the simple past verbs.

1. do   d _i_ d
2. drive   dr ____ ve
3. eat   ____ te
4. go   w ____ nt
5. have   h ____ d

6. make   m ____ de
7. read   r ____ ____ d
8. see   s ____ w
9. sleep   sl ____ pt
10. write   wr ____ te

2 Complete the conversations. Use words from Exercise 1.

1. **A** When did John _____go_____ to the hospital?

   B He _____went_____ last weekend.

2. **A** What did they _____ for dinner last night?

   B They _____ spaghetti.

3. **A** What did you _____ last weekend?

   B We _____ to the beach.

4. **A** Did he _____ a note to his sister?

   B Yes, he did.

5. **A** What did she _____ to Los Angeles last week?

   B She _____ the truck.

6. **A** What did you _____ at the library yesterday?

   B I _____ some newspapers.

7. **A** Did they _____ late last Saturday?

   B Yes, they did.

8. **A** Who did she _____ at school?

   B She _____ her friend.

Check your answers. See page 139.

3 Complete the sentences. Use the simple past.

April 7, 2008

Last week, we went on vacation. On Saturday, we _____went hiking_____. On Sunday,
                                                    1. go hiking

we _____ . On Monday, we _____ . On Tuesday,
        2. go picnicking   3. go swimming

we _____ . On Wednesday, we _____ . On Thursday, we
        4. read books   5. sleep late

_____ . On Friday night, we _____ .
    6. go fishing   7. drink hot chocolate

4 Look at the paragraph in Exercise 3. Write questions or answers.

1. _What did they do last week?_ _____

   They went on vacation.

2. _____

   They went hiking.

3. _____

   They went picnicking.

4. What did they do on Monday?

   _____

5. _____

   They read books.

6. What did they do on Wednesday?

   _____

7. _____

   They went fishing.

8. What did they do on Friday night?

   _____

Check your answers. See page 139.

What are you going to do?

Study the chart on page 126.

1 Read the Serrano family's schedule. Answer the questions.

Monday	Tuesday	Wednesday
play basketball	play soccer	buy clothes
Thursday	**Friday**	**Saturday**
drive to a lake	watch a movie	go to a party

1. What is the Serrano family going to do on Saturday?

   They are going to go to a party.

2. What are Mrs. Serrano and the children going to do on Tuesday?

   _____

3. What are Mr. and Mrs. Serrano going to do on Friday night?

   _____

4. What is Mrs. Serrano going to do on Thursday?

   _____

5. What are Mr. Serrano and the children going to do on Monday?

   _____

6. What are Mrs. Serrano and the children going to do on Wednesday?

   _____

Check your answers. See page 139.

2 Write sentences. Use *be going to*.

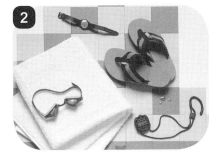

She 's *going to go* _____ (go) fishing next weekend.

He _____ (go) swimming this afternoon.

They _____ _____ (play) soccer tonight.

We _____ _____ (take) a trip next week.

I _____ _____ (clean) the house tomorrow.

She _____ _____ (buy) a house next year.

3 Complete the sentences.

1. **A** What's Chris going to do today?

   B He's *going to go swimming* _____ . (go swimming)

2. **A** What's Jim going to do tomorrow?

   B He's _____ . (go shopping)

3. **A** What are Hirori and Ross going to do tonight?

   B They're _____ . (cook dinner)

4. **A** What's Sue going to do next week?

   B She's _____ . (take a vacation)

5. **A** What's Shane going to do today?

   B He's _____ . (rest)

Check your answers. See page 139.

Lesson D Reading

1 Which words go with *go* or *play*? Write the words.

baseball	camping	football	ice hockey	soccer
basketball	fishing	hiking	skiing	swimming

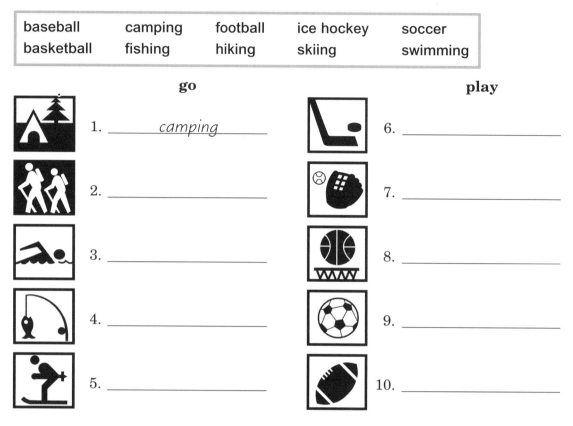

go

1. _____camping_____

2. _____

3. _____

4. _____

5. _____

play

6. _____

7. _____

8. _____

9. _____

10. _____

2 Complete the sentences. Use the simple past.

Last Saturday, the Chan family ____was____ very busy. On Saturday
                      1. be

morning, Mr. Chan _____ his family to the park. Mrs. Chan
                2. drive

_____ a walk in the park with her friend. Mr. Chan _____ his
  3. take   4. watch

daughter, Amy, play soccer. After the game, the family _____ lunch at
                                         5. eat

home. In the afternoon, they _____ some work around the house. Mrs.
                       6. do

Chan _____ tired, so she _____ a nap. Mr. Chan _____
    7. be   8. take   9. watch

ice hockey on television. Amy _____ shopping with her friends. On
                      10. go

Saturday night, they _____ dinner at a Mexican restaurant.
                11. eat

Check your answers. See page 139.

3 Read about Raul's vacation. Answer the questions.

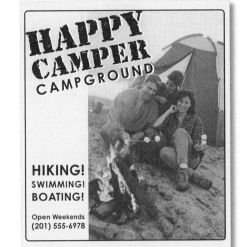

Summer Vacation

This summer I went camping with friends. We stayed at a campground. We went fishing in the morning. Every day we ate fish for lunch! In the afternoon, we went hiking. After hiking, we went swimming in the lake to relax. We went to bed late, and we got up early in the morning. We talked to other campers and made new friends. We had a great time.

HIKING!
SWIMMING!
BOATING!

Open Weekends
(201) 555-6978

1. What did Raul do this summer?

   He went camping with friends.

2. What did they do in the morning?

   _____

3. What did they eat for lunch?

   _____

4. What did they do in the afternoon?

   _____

5. Where did they go swimming?

   _____

6. When did they go to bed?

   _____

4 Number the sentences in the correct order.

_____ Finally, they're going to go to bed, tired but happy in their new home.

_____ In the morning, they're going to put boxes and furniture into a truck.

_____ At 6:00 p.m., they're going to go to a restaurant to celebrate.

_____ Then, they're going to drive the truck to their new house.

_____ In the afternoon, they're going to bring the boxes and furniture into their new house.

_1_ Tomorrow, the Velasco family is moving out of their apartment and into a new house.

Check your answers. See page 139.

Writing

1 Write a conversation. Use the sentences in the box.

Speaker A	Speaker B
Who is the party for?	I'm going to go to a birthday party.
What are you going to do this weekend?	Yes, I'm going to have a lot of fun.
That sounds like fun.	It's my sister's birthday.

1. **A** *What are you going to do this weekend?*
2. **B** _____
3. **A** _____
4. **B** _____
5. **A** _____
6. **B** _____

2 Write sentences.

1. What / last weekend / do / did / you / ?
   What did you do last weekend?

2. in the mountains / went hiking / We / .

   _____

3. go / Did / you / with your son / ?

   _____

4. No, / a friend / went / with / I / .

   _____

5. swimming / go / Did / you / ?

   _____

6. canoeing / Yes, / we / went swimming / and / .

   _____

7. next weekend / to do / What / you / are / going / ?

   _____

Check your answers. See page 139.

3 Read the paragraph. Add capital letters.

> *A*
> ~~a~~li had a good weekend. On Saturday, he went to a
> baseball game with his friend. they ate hot dogs and drank
> sodas. they came home at 5:00. on Sunday, ali played
> soccer with his friends at the park near his house. they
> played all afternoon. they had a good time.

4 Correct the sentences.

went
1. I ~~go~~ to the park last weekend.

2. Maria drive to the shopping mall yesterday.

3. Ali and Miriam eat Chinese food last weekend.

4. John play soccer last weekend.

5. What do you going to do next Friday?

6. Is he go to go to the concert on Sunday?

7. He ride the bus to the concert next Sunday.

5 Rewrite the paragraph. Change *Susanna* to *Susanna and Maria*.

>   Susanna is going to go camping
> on Saturday. She needs some food.
> She is going to buy some bread, milk,
> and eggs. Then she is going to drive
> to the beach. In the afternoon, she
> is going to go hiking. On Sunday
> morning, she is going to go swimming
> and fishing. She likes to exercise.

Susanna and Maria are going to go camping on Saturday. They _____

_____

_____

_____

Check your answers. See page 139.

Another view

1 Look at the ad. Answer the questions.

SAN DIEGO CITY FAIR

Del Mar Fairgrounds
San Diego, California
June 16–July 5
Fireworks: July 4
Hot-dog-eating contest: June 23

Hours: 10 a.m. to 10 p.m., Sundays through Thursdays
10 a.m. to 11 p.m., Fridays and Saturdays

Admission: Adults: $10.50
Seniors 62 and older: $6
Children 6–12: $4.50
Children 5 and younger: free

Discounts: Every Tuesday, children 12 and younger get in free. Free parking, with free shuttle bus to fairgrounds.
Information: (858) 555-1161

1. When does the fair start?
   a. June 16
   b. June 23
   c. July 4
   d. July 5

2. How much is a ticket for a 10-year-old on a Tuesday?
   a. $6.00
   b. $4.50
   c. $10.50
   d. It's free.

3. When is the hot-dog-eating contest?
   a. June 16
   b. June 23
   c. July 4
   d. July 5

4. When does the fair end?
   a. June 16
   b. June 24
   c. July 4
   d. July 5

5. How much is parking?
   a. $7
   b. $10.50
   c. $13
   d. It's free.

6. When does the fair close on Saturday nights?
   a. 9:00 p.m.
   b. 10:00 p.m.
   c. 11:00 p.m.
   d. midnight

Check your answers. See page 140.

2 Complete the chart.

in two days	last year	tonight	next weekend
two weeks ago	in two weeks	last night	last month
one week ago	last week	in one month	next week
tomorrow	yesterday	last weekend	last Saturday

Simple past: I went fishing.	Future: I am going to go fishing.
one week ago	in two days

3 Complete the sentences. Use the correct form of *play* or *go*.

1. Yesterday, he ____*played*____ soccer.

2. They are going to _____ baseball tonight.

3. I _____ skiing last weekend.

4. Last night, they _____ dancing.

5. We are going to _____ shopping this afternoon.

6. He is going to _____ basketball with his friends tomorrow.

7. I _____ picnicking in the park last weekend.

8. He is going to _____ surfing next weekend.

9. The children _____ fishing a week ago.

10. Are you _____ ice-skating tonight?

Check your answers. See page 140.

Reference charts

Present of *be*

Affirmative statements

I'm	
You're	
He's	
She's	
It's	from Somalia.
We're	
You're	
They're	

I'm	=	I am
You're	=	You are
He's	=	He is
She's	=	She is
It's	=	It is
We're	=	We are
You're	=	You are
They're	=	They are

Yes / No questions

Am	I	
Are	you	
Is	he	
Is	she	
Is	it	from Guatemala?
Are	we	
Are	you	
Are	they	

Short answers

Yes,	you are.	No,	you aren't.
	I am.		I'm not.
	he is.		he isn't.
	she is.		she isn't.
	it is.		it isn't.
	you are.		you aren't.
	we are.		we aren't.
	they are.		they aren't.

Present continuous

Affirmative statements

I'm	
You're	
He's	
She's	
It's	eating.
We're	
You're	
They're	

Yes / No questions

Am	I	
Are	you	
Is	he	
Is	she	
Is	it	eating?
Are	we	
Are	you	
Are	they	

Short answers

Yes,	you are.	No,	you aren't.
	I am.		I'm not.
	he is.		he isn't.
	she is.		she isn't.
	it is.		it isn't.
	you are.		you aren't.
	we are.		we aren't.
	they are.		they aren't.

Wh- questions

	am	I	
	are	you	
	is	he	
	is	she	
What	is	it	doing?
	is	it	
	are	we	
	are	you	
	are	they	

Answers

You're	
I'm	
He's	
She's	
It's	eating.
You're	
We're	
They're	

Possessive adjectives

What's	my your his her its our your their	address?

Your My His Her Its Your Our Their	address is 10 Main Street.

Simple present

Affirmative statements

I	work.
You	work.
He	works.
She	works.
It	works.
We	work.
You	work.
They	work.

Negative statements

I	don't	
You	don't	
He	doesn't	
She	doesn't	work.
It	doesn't	
We	don't	
You	don't	
They	don't	

Yes / No questions

Do	I	
Do	you	
Does	he	
Does	she	work?
Does	it	
Do	we	
Do	you	
Do	they	

Short answers

Yes,	you	do.
	I	do.
	he	does.
	she	does.
	it	does.
	you	do.
	we	do.
	they	do.

No,	you	don't.
	I	don't.
	he	doesn't.
	she	doesn't.
	it	doesn't.
	you	don't.
	we	don't.
	they	don't.

Wh- questions

What	do do does does does do do do	I you he she it we you they	do at 7:00?

Answers

You	work.
I	work.
He	works.
She	works.
It	works.
You	work.
We	work.
They	work.

Simple present of *have*

Affirmative statements

I	have	a cold.
You	have	a cold.
He	has	a cold.
She	has	a cold.
It	has	a cold.
We	have	colds.
You	have	colds.
They	have	colds.

Negative statements

I	don't have	a cold.
You	don't have	a cold.
He	doesn't have	a cold.
She	doesn't have	a cold.
It	doesn't have	a cold.
We	don't have	colds.
You	don't have	colds.
They	don't have	colds.

Yes / No questions

Do	I		a cold?
Do	you		a cold?
Does	he		a cold?
Does	she	have	a cold?
Does	it		a cold?
Do	we		colds?
Do	you		colds?
Do	they		colds?

Short answers

Yes,	you	do.	No,	you	don't.
	I	do.		I	don't.
	he	does.		he	doesn't.
	she	does.		she	doesn't.
	it	does.		it	doesn't.
	you	do.		you	don't.
	we	do.		we	don't.
	they	do.		they	don't.

Simple past of *be*

Affirmative statements

I	was	a teacher.
You	were	a teacher.
He	was	a teacher.
She	was	a teacher.
We	were	teachers.
You	were	teachers.
They	were	teachers.

Negative statements

I	wasn't	a cashier.
You	weren't	a cashier.
He	wasn't	a cashier.
She	wasn't	a cashier.
We	weren't	cashiers.
You	weren't	cashiers.
They	weren't	cashiers.

Yes / No questions

Was	I	a teacher?
Were	you	a teacher?
Was	he	a teacher?
Was	she	a teacher?
Were	we	teachers?
Were	you	teachers?
Were	they	teachers?

Short answers

Yes,	you	were.	No,	you	weren't.
	I	was.		I	wasn't.
	he	was.		he	wasn't.
	she	was.		she	wasn't.
	you	were.		you	weren't.
	we	were.		we	weren't.
	they	were.		they	weren't.

Simple past of regular and irregular verbs

Affirmative statements

I You He She It We You They	cooked. slept.

Negative statements

I You He She It We You They	didn't	cook. sleep.

Yes / No questions

Did	I you he she it we you they	cook? sleep?

Short answers

Yes,	you I he she it you we they	did.

No,	you I he she it you we they	didn't.

Wh- questions

What	did	I you he she it we you they	do?

Answers

You I He She It You We They	cooked. slept.

Regular verbs

Add -ed: cook → cooked   talk → talked
          dust → dusted   wash → washed

Irregular verbs

break → broke	get → got	ride → rode	sweep → swept
buy → bought	go → went	run → ran	swim → swam
do → did	have → had	see → saw	take → took
drink → drank	make → made	sell → sold	wear → wore
drive → drove	pay → paid	sit → sat	write → wrote
eat → ate	read → read	sleep → slept	

Can

I You He She It We You They	can	help.

Negative statements

I You He She It We You They	can't	help.

Yes / No questions

Can	I you he she it we you they	help?

Short answers

Yes,	you I he she it you we they	can.

No,	you I he she it you we they	can't.

Future – *be going to*

Affirmative statements

I'm You're He's She's It's We're You're They're	going to	play.

Negative statements

I'm You're He's She's It's We're You're They're	not going to	play.

Wh- questions

What	am I are you is he is she is it are we are you are they	going to do tomorrow?

Answers

You're I'm He's She's It's You're We're They're	going to	play.

Unit 1: Personal information

Lesson A: Get ready

Exercise 1 page 2

1. first
2. middle
3. last
4. telephone
5. area
6. zip

Exercise 2 page 2

1. first name
2. area code
3. last name
4. telephone number
5. middle name
6. zip code

Exercise 3 page 3

1. b   3. d   5. c
2. e   4. a

Exercise 4 page 3

1. last name
2. first name
3. address
4. area code
5. telephone number

Exercise 5 page 3

1. (631) 555-7810
2. (642) 555-1972
3. (432) 555-9803
4. (798) 555-6421

Lesson B: What's your name?

Exercise 1 page 4

1. f   3. h   5. b   7. d
2. c   4. a   6. g   8. e

Exercise 2 page 4

1A. his   3A. her
1B. His   3B. Her
2A. his   4A. their
2B. His   4B. Their

Exercise 3 page 4

1. b   2. b   3. b

Exercise 4 page 5

1A. his   3A. their
1B. His   3B. Their
2A. her
2B. Her

Exercise 5 page 5

1. His name is John Brown-Hudson.
2. Her first name is Mary.
3. Their last name is Lopez.
4. His area code is 608.
5. Their zip code is 02455.
6. Her telephone number is 555-1234.

Lesson C: Are you from Canada?

Exercise 1 page 6

1. We're
2. They're
3. He's
4. She's
5. I'm
6. They're

Exercise 2 page 6

1. She's from Ecuador.
2. He's from Chile.
3. He isn't from Honduras.
4. They're from Colombia.
5. You're from the Ukraine.
6. They're from Pakistan.
7. They aren't from Poland.
8. She isn't from Peru.
9. You aren't from Vietnam.
10. She's from El Salvador.

Exercise 3 page 7

1. No, he isn't.
2. Yes, he is.
3. No, she isn't.
4. Yes, she is.
5. No, I'm not.
6. Yes, I am.
7. No, they aren't.
8. Yes, they are.

Exercise 4 page 7

1A. is   4A. are
1B. is   4B. are
2A. Are   5A. is
2B. am   5B. is
3A. Is   6A. is
3B. is   6B. is

Lesson D: Reading

Exercise 1 page 8

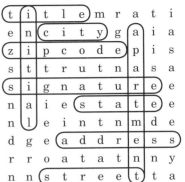

Exercise 2 page 8

1. title   6. city
2. initial   7. state
3. address   8. zip code
4. street   9. signature
5. apartment

Exercise 3 page 9

1. a   3. a   5. b
2. a   4. b   6. b

Exercise 4 page 9

Name:
Cabrera   _Juan_   _Carlos_
Last   First   Middle
Address:
138 Clark Avenue, Apt. 6
Tampa,   _Florida_   _33629_
City   State   Zip
Phone:
(_813_) _555_ - _3461_

Lesson E: Writing

Exercise 1 page 10

1. They are from China.
2. Where are you from?
3. Mary is her middle name.
4. What is her last name?
5. How do you spell that?
6. His address is 1241 Washington Avenue.
7. What is your telephone number?
8. Their area code is 202.

Exercise 2 page 10

1. His name is Bill Jackson.
2. He is a new student.
3. His address is 371 Purdy Avenue.
4. His telephone number is 555-7819.
5. He is from New York.

Exercise 3 page 11

1. last name
2. area code
3. zip code
4. telephone number
5. address
6. middle initial

Exercise 4 page 11

1. I'm Terri.
2. Hi, Terri. What's your last name?
3. My last name is Smith.
4. OK, what's your telephone number?
5. My telephone number is (545) 555-7771.
6. Thanks. We'll call you soon.

Lesson F: Another view

Exercise 1 page 12

1 Sue
2. Valley Adult School
3. 91109
4. V00-82496
5. Hudson Avenue
6. L.
7. Pasadena
8. Chang
9. 4A

Exercise 2 page 12

1. b   2. b   3. a   4. b

Exercise 3 page 13

Down

1. country   5. state
2. middle   8. title
4. last

Across

3. zip   7. apartment
6. address   9. city

Unit 2: At school

Lesson A: Get ready

Exercise 1 page 14

1. calculator
2. book
3. pencil
4. map
5. table
6. clock
7. desk
8. eraser
9. notebook
10. ruler

Exercise 2 page 14

1. clock
2. map
3. book
4. calculator
5. table
6. eraser
7. notebook
8. ruler
9. desk
10. pencil

Exercise 3 page 15

On the desks

eraser
notebook
pencil
ruler

On the table

book
calculator

Exercise 4 page 15

1. c   2. b   3. c   4. a

Lesson B: Where is the pen?

Exercise 1 page 16

1. computer, on
2. eraser, in
3. ruler, in
4. calendar, on
5. dictionary, on
6. calculator, in

Exercise 2 page 16

1. a   2. a   3. b   4. b

Exercise 3 page 17

1A. Where are the calculators?
1B. They're on the table.
2A. Where's the calendar?
2B. It's in the cabinet.
3A. Where are the books?
3B. They're in the cabinet.
4A. Where's the notebook?
4B. It's on the table.

Exercise 4 page 17

3   5   1   6   4   2

Exercise 5 page 17

1A. Where's the pencil?
1B. It's on the table.
2A. Where's the calendar?
2B. It's on the wall.
3A. Where's the eraser?
3B. It's on the desk.

4A. Where's the ruler?
4B. It's in the box.
5A. Where's the calculator?
5B. It's in the drawer.
6A. Where's the pen?
6B. It's on the table.

Lesson C: Where are the pencils?

Exercise 1 page 18

1. bookcase
2. dictionary
3. notebooks
4. desks
5. erasers
6. rulers
7. pencils
8. map
9. clocks
10. telephones
11. calendar
12. boxes
13. cabinet
14. calculator

Exercise 2 page 19

Singular nouns

bookcase
cabinet
calculator
calendar
dictionary
map

Plural nouns

boxes
clocks
desks
erasers
notebooks
pencils
rulers
telephones

Exercise 3 page 19

1. they are
2. it isn't
3. they are
4. it is
5. they aren't
6. it isn't
7. they are
8. they are
9. it isn't
10. they are

Exercise 4 page 19

1A. Where are the dictionaries?
1B. They are on the shelf.
2A. Is the book on the table?
2B. No, it isn't.
3A. Is the pencil in the desk drawer?
3B. Yes, it is.

Lesson D: Reading

Exercise 1 page 20

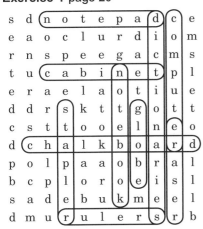

Exercise 2 page 20

1. f	3. e	5. d
2. b	4. a	6. c

Exercise 3 page 21

1. May I help you?
2. Yes, please. Where are the notebooks?
3. The notebooks are on the top shelf.
4. Thanks. I also need a pencil.
5. Pencils are on the bottom shelf.
6. Great. Now I'm ready to write!

Exercise 4 page 21

1. The notepads are in the desk drawer.
2. The pencils are in a box on the shelf.
3. The erasers are in the box, too.
4. The dictionaries are in the bookcase.
5. The stapler is on the desk.

Lesson E: Writing

Exercise 1 page 22

1. Where are the books?
2. The pencil sharpener is on the wall.
3. Are the books on the shelf?
4. The pencils are on the desk.
5. Is the teacher in the classroom?
6. Where is the computer?
7. The notebook is on the desk.
8. Is the stapler in the drawer?

Exercise 2 page 23

1. it is
2. they aren't
3. it is
4. they are
5. it isn't
6. it is
7. they are
8. it is
9. it isn't

Exercise 3 page 23

1. The classroom is ready for the students.
2. The books are in the bookcase.
3. The map is on the wall.
4. The globe is on the filing cabinet.
5. The pencils are on the table.
6. The teacher's name is on the chalkboard.
7. The markers are in the drawer.
8. The calculators are on the bookcase.

Lesson F: Another view

Exercise 1 page 24

1. a	3. b	5. d	7. a
2. b	4. c	6. d	8. c

Exercise 2 page 25

Down	Across
1. globe	2. chalk
3. eraser	4. index cards
5. chalkboard	9. computer
6. calculator	10. paper clips
7. ruler	11. notepad
8. stapler	

Unit 3: Friends and family

Lesson A: Get ready

Exercise 1 page 26

1. grandfather
2. grandmother
3. sister
4. brother
5. mother
6. father

Exercise 2 page 26

1. wife
2. son
3. daughter
4. mother
5. grandfather

Exercise 3 page 27

1. 212
2. 07480
3. (201) 555-1850
4. Chen
5. (973) 555-1972
6. Honolulu, HI
7. Jones
8. 40 West 20th Street

Lesson B: What are you doing?

Exercise 1 page 28

1. He's cleaning his room.
2. He's studying English.
3. He's helping his dad.
4. He's watching his little sister.
5. He's washing dishes.

Exercise 2 page 28

1. 's cleaning
2. 's talking
3. 's playing
4. 's eating
5. 's watching
6. 's listening
7. 's studying
8. 's drinking

Exercise 3 page 29

is celebrating
is sleeping
is cooking
is cleaning
is helping

Exercise 4 page 29

1. Hello?
2. Hi, Margie. How are you?

3. I'm OK. What are you doing?
4. I'm taking a break. Are you busy?
5. Yes, I'm cooking dinner.
6. What are the children doing?
7. They're doing their homework.
8. That's good. See you soon.

Lesson C: Are you working now?

Exercise 1 page 30
1. Yes, she is.
2. No, he isn't.
3. No, he isn't.
4. Yes, he is.
5. Yes, she is.
6. Yes, he is.
7. No, they aren't.
8. No, they aren't.

Exercise 2 page 30
1. She is cleaning the house.
2. She is listening to music.
3. He is talking on the telephone.
4. He is reading a newspaper.
5. He is reading a book.

Exercise 3 page 31
1. Is she cleaning the house?
2. Is she listening to music?
3. Is he talking on the telephone?
4. Is he reading a newspaper?
5. Is he reading?

Exercise 4 page 31
1. is drinking
2. is studying
3. is cooking
4. is helping
5. are watching

Lesson D: Reading

Exercise 1 page 32

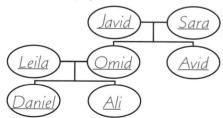

Exercise 2 page 32
1. husband
2. mother
3. wife
4. sister

5. brother
6. grandson
7. daughter
8. son
9. grandfather
10. grandmother

Exercise 3 page 33
1. grandmother
2. grandfather
3. sister-in-law
4. uncle
5. sister
6. niece
7. nephew
8. cousin

Exercise 4 page 33
1. Hello? This is Susan.
2. Hi, Susan. This is Ann. What are you doing?
3. I'm studying for the English test.
4. Oh, no! I forgot about the test.
5. Don't worry. It isn't a big test.
6. That's good. Talk to you later.
7. OK. See you tomorrow, Ann.

Lesson E: Writing

Exercise 1 page 34
1A. What are you doing?
1B. I'm cooking for my family.
2A. How many brothers do you have?
2B. I have two brothers.
3A. Do you have any sisters?
3B. I have five sisters.

Exercise 2 page 34
1. Today is Ana's birthday.
2. She is 15 years old.
3. Ana's mother, Luisa, is making a birthday cake.
4. Her grandparents are wrapping presents.
5. Ana is having a big party.
6. Her friends are dancing at the party.
7. Ana's father, Reynaldo, is taking pictures.
8. They are very happy today.

Exercise 3 page 35
1. We're having
2. They're talking
3. They're singing

4. She's cooking
5. He's taking

Exercise 4 page 35
1. I am married. I have one daughter.
2. Her name is Paula.
3. She is 10 years old today.
4. She is having a party with her friends.
5. They are playing outside now.
6. She is happy.

Lesson F: Another view

Exercise 1 page 36
1. grandmother
2. grandfather
3. aunt
4. uncle
5. mother
6. father
7. cousin
8. sister

Exercise 2 page 36
1. son
2. daughter
3. mother
4. watching
5. music
6. TV
7. guitar
8. friend

Exercise 3 page 37
1. b   2. b   3. c   4. a

Exercise 4 page 37
1. Chicago
2. Clarkson
3. Bianca
4. June 2, 2006

Unit 4: Health

Lesson A: Get ready

Exercise 1 page 38

```
a n k l e  a  e  a  r
s o r e  t  k  c  c  m
t s r a h t  t  o  h  s
f e v e r  b  u  h  n
o a e d o  a  g  h  h
s t o m a c  h  t  e
a t h k t  k  r  a  a
a t e a s e e  d  d
s c o l d  s  c  f  o
```

Exercise 2 page 38

Parts of the body

ankle

back

ear

head

stomach

Problems

ache

cold

cough

fever

sore

Exercise 3 page 38

1. c   2. d   3. a   4. b

Exercise 4 page 39

1. headache
2. stomachache
3. broken leg
4. backache
5. earache
6. sore throat
7. cough
8. fever
9. sprained ankle

Lesson B: I have a headache.

Exercise 1 page 40

1. c   2. a   3. b   4. d

Exercise 2 page 40

1. have
2. has
3. has
4. have
5. have
6. have

Exercise 3 page 41

1. He has a broken arm.
2. She has a sore throat.
3. He has a backache.
4. He has a sprained ankle.
5. They have colds.
6. She has a stomachache.

Exercise 4 page 41

1. How are you?
2. I'm tired, and I'm hot.
3. Do you have a fever?
4. Yes, I do. Do you have aspirin?
5. Yes, I do. I have aspirin and vitamin C.
6. Thank you.

Lesson C: Do you have a cold?

Exercise 1 page 42

1. a   3. b   5. a
2. a   4. b

Exercise 2 page 42

1. has
2. He
3. doesn't
4. has
5. doesn't
6. does

Exercise 3 page 42

1B. him   3B. him
1A. He   3A. He
2B. her   4B. her
2A. She   4A. She

Exercise 4 page 43

1. Does she have a stomachache?
2. Does he have a sore throat?
3. Does he have a broken leg?
4. Do they have colds?
5. Do you have a cough?
6. Do you have a fever?
7. Does she have an earache?
8. Do you have a cut?
9. Does she have a sprained ankle?
10. Do they have headaches?

Lesson D: Reading

Exercise 1 page 44

1. toe   7. finger
2. nose   8. foot
3. ankle   9. knee
4. eye   10. tooth
5. chin   11. ear
6. hand   12. stomach

Exercise 2 page 44

1. eye   4. stomach
2. ankle   5. knee
3. hand   6. ear

Exercise 3 page 45

2   6   4   1   5   3

Exercise 4 page 45

1. The Simon family is at the doctor's office.
2. Bobby has a sore arm.
3. Margaret has a cold and a sore throat.
4. Yes, the baby has a fever.
5. Mr. and Mrs. Simon are tired!

Lesson E: Writing

Exercise 1 page 46

1. October 4, 2008
2. Mr. Rodriguez
3. Sarah Johnson
4. sore throat and a fever
5. Rita Johnson

Exercise 2 page 46

Dear Miss Nguyen,

Debra Garcia is my niece. She isn't in school today. She is at home. She has a cold and a fever. Please excuse her.

Thank you,

Jerry Garcia

Exercise 3 page 47

Jim Garcia is my nephew. He isn't in school today. He is at home. He has a cold and a fever. Please excuse him.

Exercise 4 page 47

6   5   1   3   2   4

Lesson F: Another view

Exercise 1 page 48

One

back   nose

chin   stomach

head   throat

neck

A pair (two)

ankle   hand

arm   knee

ear   leg

eye   shoulder

foot   wrist

More than two

finger

toe

tooth

Exercise 2 page 48

1. stomachache
2. cough
3. sore throat
4. fever
5. headache
6. earache

Exercise 3 page 49

1. Soon-Mi Won
2. Wednesday, August 1, at 3:45 p.m.
3. Jack Murphy, MD
4. 1875 Pacific Coast Highway
5. (562) 555-4924
6. (562) 555-2034

Exercise 4 page 49

1. Yes   3. No   5. Yes
2. Yes   4. No

Unit 5: Around town

Lesson A: Get ready

Exercise 1 page 50

1. restaurant
2. hospital
3. bus stop
4. drugstore

Exercise 2 page 50

1. museum
2. hospital
3. library
4. grocery store

Exercise 3 page 51

1. restaurant
2. house
3. museum
4. bus stop
5. hospital
6. drugstore
7. library
8. post office
9. grocery store

Exercise 4 page 51

1. restaurant
2. library
3. hospital
4. school

Lesson B: It's on the corner.

Exercise 1 page 52

1. next to
2. across from
3. on the corner of
4. between
5. next to
6. on the corner of
7. on
8. across from

Exercise 2 page 53

1. It's on the corner of Belmont Avenue and Second Street.
2. It's on Belmont Avenue.
3. It's next to the hospital.
4. It's on the corner of Belmont Avenue and Second Street.
5. It's next to the library.
6. It's on Belmont Avenue.
7. It's across from the post office.
8. It's between the coffee shop and the bank.
9. It's on the corner of Belmont Avenue and Maple Street.
10. It's across from the grocery store.

Exercise 3 page 53

1. Where's the school?
2. Where's the hospital?
3. Where's the parking lot?
4. Where's the bus stop?
5. Where's the library?
6. Where's the art museum?
7. Where's the grocery store?
8. Where's the restaurant?

Lesson C: Go two blocks.

Exercise 1 page 54

1. post office
2. hospital
3. grocery store
4. bus station
5. park

Exercise 2 page 55

1. coffee shop
2. Indian restaurant
3. post office
4. bus station
5. hospital
6. museum
7. park

Lesson D: Reading

Exercise 1 page 56

Places for children
day-care center
high school
playground

Places for food
coffee shop
grocery store
restaurant

Places for help
hospital
police station

Exercise 2 page 56

1. apartment building
2. high school
3. shopping mall
4. hospital
5. day-care center

Exercise 3 page 56

1. Excuse me, where's the post office?
2. It's on the corner of Fifth and Union.
3. It's on the corner of Sixth and Union?
4. No, on Fifth and Union.
5. OK, Fifth and Union. Is it next to the bank?
6. Yes, it's next to the bank.

Exercise 4 page 57

1. He's in Los Angeles.
2. He's eating lunch at a Mexican restaurant and writing postcards.
3. He's writing to Mary Ann.
4. It's about five blocks from the restaurant.
5. It's next to the post office.

Exercise 5 page 57

1. It's across from her children's school.
2. It's next to Lin's apartment.
3. He walks to work.
4. Yes, it's very good.

Lesson E: Writing

Exercise 1 page 58

1. Where's the train station?
2. The grocery store is on the corner of Broadway and Main.
3. How do I get to the shopping mall?
4. It's next to the train station.
5. Turn left on Maple Street.

Exercise 2 page 58

1. Turn left on Maple Street.
2. The grocery store is on the corner of Broadway and Main.
3. Where's the train station?

4. How do I get to the shopping mall?
5. It's next to the train station.

Exercise 3 page 59

Janet lives at 3725 Delta Street. She goes to school at Madison Adult School. She walks down Delta Street for three blocks and turns right on Skyline Drive. She goes two blocks and turns left on National Avenue. The school is at 3500 National Avenue, next to Bandini Bakery.

Exercise 4 page 59

1. She lives on Main Street.
2. There is a library between the restaurant and the bank.
3. Go straight on Main Street.
4. It's next to the school.
5. Turn left on Main Street.
6. The coffee shop is across from the school.

Exercise 5 page 59

1. between
2. across
3. turns
4. turns
5. on
6. on the corner of

Lesson F: Another view

Exercise 1 page 60

1. menu
2. teacher
3. gas
4. museum
5. dictionaries
6. classrooms

Exercise 2 page 60

Down
1. park
3. library
5. museum
Across
2. school
4. DMV
6. bank
7. hospital
8. house

Exercise 3 page 61

1. d   3. d   5. c
2. a   4. a   6. b

Unit 6: Time

Lesson A: Get ready

Exercise 1 page 62

1. c   3. b   5. f
2. e   4. d   6. a

Exercise 2 page 62

1. take a break
2. read a schedule
3. catch the bus
4. buy a snack
5. get home
6. leave for work

Exercise 3 page 63

1. f   3. i   5. c   7. a   9. h
2. j   4. d   6. g   8. e   10. b

Exercise 4 page 63

1. 12:00   5. 6:00
2. 8:45   6. 8:25
3. 3:45   7. 5:30
4. 4:20   8. 11:00

Exercise 5 page 63

1. six-ten
2. ten-forty
3. two-twenty-five
4. nine-fifty
5. twelve-oh-five
6. seven-fifteen
7. eleven-fifty-five
8. one-thirty-five

Lesson B: What do you do in the evening?

Exercise 1 page 64

1A. do
1B. go, study
2A. does
2B. plays
3B. goes
4A. does
4B. watches
5B. read, exercise

Exercise 2 page 64

1. What do you do at night?
2. I usually go to class.
3. Where's your class?
4. It's at the Washington Community School.
5. Do you study English?
6. Yes, I do.

Exercise 3 page 65

1. study
2. watches
3. exercises
4. listen
5. work

Exercise 4 page 65

1. What do you do in the morning?
2. What do you do in the evening?
3. What do you do in the afternoon?
4. What do you do on Saturday?

Lesson C: I go to work at 8:00.

Exercise 1 page 66

at
eight-thirty
eleven
night
in
the evening
June
the morning
on
Monday
Thursday afternoon
Wednesday night

Exercise 2 page 66

1. at
2. at, on
3. at, in, on
4. at, on, at, on

Exercise 3 page 67

1. The meeting is at 5:30 p.m.
2. It's on Saturday.
3. It starts at 7:00 a.m.
4. It ends at 10:00 a.m.
5. It's on Saturday.
6. It starts at 2:00 p.m.
7. It ends at 6:00.
8. It's on January 5.

Lesson D: Reading

Exercise 1 page 68

1. c   2. a   3. d   4. a

Exercise 2 page 68

1. He works at a restaurant.
2. He leaves for work early in the morning.
3. He gets ready to cook dinner.
4. He goes home late at night.

Exercise 3 page 69

eat
breakfast
dinner
lunch

go
shopping
to bed
to work

take
a break
the children to school
a shower

Exercise 4 page 69

1A. eat lunch
1B. They eat lunch at 12 o'clock.
2A. take a break
2B. They take a break at 3:30.
3A. go to work
3B. He goes to work at 8 o'clock.
4A. go to bed
4B. She goes to bed at 10 o'clock.

Lesson E: Writing

Exercise 1 page 70

1. When does she volunteer?
2. What time does she go to work?
3. What do you do on the weekend?
4. Does he go to the park on Saturday morning?
5. What time do your children go to bed?
6. When does he walk the dog?

Exercise 2 page 70

1. When does she volunteer?
2. When does he walk the dog?
3. What do you do on the weekend?
4. What time do your children go to bed?
5. What time does she go to work?
6. Does he go to the park on Saturday morning?

Exercise 3 page 71

1. Susie works at the library, and she goes to school.
2. She works on Monday, Wednesday, and Friday.
3. She begins work at 9:00 a.m.
4. She has lunch from 12:00 to 1:00 p.m.
5. She finishes work at 5:00 p.m.
6. On Tuesday and Thursday, she doesn't work. She goes to school.

Exercise 4 page 71

1. On
2. at
3. in
4. At
5. in
6. at
7. in
8. On
9. On

Lesson F: Another view

Exercise 1 page 72

1. Sunday
2. Monday
3. Tuesday
4. Wednesday
5. Thursday
6. Friday
7. Saturday

Exercise 2 page 72

1. January
2. February
3. March
4. April
5. August
6. September
7. October
8. November
9. December

Exercise 3 page 72

1. a movie
2. the radio
3. a newspaper
4. homework
5. bed
6. the park
7. English
8. TV
9. January
10. a soccer game

Exercise 4 page 73

1. a
2. a
3. d
4. b
5. c
6. d

Unit 7: Shopping

Lesson A: Get ready

Exercise 1 page 74

1. apples
2. bananas
3. bread
4. cheese
5. cookies
6. milk
7. onions
8. potatoes
9. tomatoes

Exercise 2 page 74

1. milk
2. tomatoes
3. potatoes
4. cheese
5. cookies
6. bananas
7. apples
8. bread
9. onions

Exercise 3 page 75

1. bananas 99¢
2. bread $1.79
3. apples $1.90
4. tomatoes $2.29
5. milk $2.49
6. cookies $2.50
7. onions $2.69
8. potatoes $2.99
9. cheese $4.00

Exercise 4 page 75

1. d
2. h
3. e
4. j
5. g
6. c
7. a
8. b
9. f
10. i

Exercise 5 page 75

1. $9.59
2. $2.25
3. $8.30
4. $5.10
5. $6.41
6. $15.99
7. $10.62
8. $20.15

Lesson B: How many? How much?

Exercise 1 page 76

How many . . . ?
apples   peaches
bananas   pies
eggs   strawberries
oranges

How much . . . ?
cheese   rice
coffee   sugar
juice   water
milk

Exercise 2 page 76

1. How many apples do you need?
2. How much sugar does she need?
3. How many strawberries do they need?
4. How many eggs do I need?
5. How much water does he need?
6. How many oranges do you need?

Exercise 3 page 77

1. Where are you going?
2. To the grocery store.
3. We need apples and juice.
4. OK. How many apples?
5. We need five or six.
6. How much juice do we need?
7. Not much.
8. OK. See you later.

Exercise 4 page 77

1. much
2. need
3. does
4. many
5. needs
6. a lot

Lesson C: Are there any bananas?

Exercise 1 page 78

1. Yes, there are.
2. No, there isn't.
3. No, there aren't.
4. Yes, there is.
5. Yes, there are.
6. Yes, there is.
7. Yes, there is.
8. No, there isn't.
9. No, there isn't.
10. Yes, there is.

Exercise 2 page 78

1. bags
2. bottle
3. cans
4. box
5. glass
6. cartons
7. loaf
8. package

Exercise 3 page 79

1. box
2. carton
3. bottle
4. package
5. can
6. bag

Exercise 4 page 79

1. d   3. c
2. d   4. b

Exercise 5 page 79

1. There are
2. There is
3. There is
4. There are
5. There are
6. There are
7. There is
8. There are

Lesson D: Reading

Exercise 1 page 80

Exercise 2 page 80

1. quarter   4. dime
2. one   5. five
3. twenty   6. ten

Exercise 3 page 81

1. grocery   4. tea
2. bread   5. rice
3. milk   6. onions

Exercise 4 page 81

1. She usually goes to the grocery store.
2. She is shopping at Best Food Market.
3. She is buying a gallon of milk.
4. She is buying a bag of rice.
5. She is buying two onions.
6. The total is $15.36.
7. She has a ten-dollar bill.
8. She is writing a check.

Lesson E: Writing

Exercise 1 page 82

1. Do we need a carton of milk?
2. Is there any juice in the refrigerator?
3. Is she buying a bottle of water?
4. Are there any bananas on the shelf?
5. How much coffee do you need?
6. How many oranges are there on the table?
7. How much money does she have in her purse?
8. What is his favorite grocery store?

Exercise 2 page 82

1. carton   4. bag
2. three   5. loaf
3. box   6. credit card

Exercise 3 page 83

1. package   5. package
2. can   6. box
3. bag   7. three
4. carton   8. one

Exercise 4 page 83

Walter is a regular customer at Happy Day Supermarket. He usually goes three times a week. Everybody knows him. Today he's buying three apples, two oranges, a package of cookies, and a can of soda. He needs to pay $8.95. Walter only has a five-dollar bill, a one-dollar bill, and a quarter. He can write a check.

Exercise 5 page 83

I am a regular customer at Happy Day Supermarket. I usually go three times a week. Everybody knows me. Today I'm buying three apples, two oranges, a package of cookies, and a can of soda. I need to pay $8.95. I only have a five-dollar bill, a one-dollar bill, and a quarter. I can write a check.

Lesson F: Another view

Exercise 1 page 84

1. July 3, 2008
2. Happy Day Supermarket
3. Walter Taylor
4. $8.95

5. Dayton Bank
6. 1702

Exercise 2 page 84

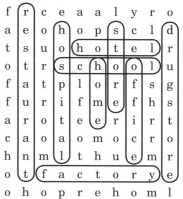

(Answers will vary)

PAY TO THE ORDER OF Acme Grocery $ 42.68
Forty-two and 68/100   DOLLARS
Dayton Bank
MEMO groceries   (Answers will vary)

Exercise 3 page 85

Across
1. much
3. half
7. groceries
8. Are
9. check
10. many
11. bottle
12. card

Down
2. change
4. nickel
5. Is
6. banana
11. bill

Unit 8: Work

Lesson A: Get ready

Exercise 1 page 86
1. busboy
2. cook
3. nurse
4. waiter
5. waitress
6. doctor
7. nursing assistant
8. cashier

Exercise 2 page 86
1. busboy, cashier, cook, waiter, waitress
2. doctor, nurse, nursing assistant

Exercise 3 page 86

1. g	3. f	5. b	7. a
2. d	4. h	6. e	8. c

Exercise 4 page 87
1. He's a busboy.
2. She's a nurse.
3. She's a cashier.
4. He's an office worker.
5. He's a construction worker.
6. She's an electrician.

7. She's a cook.
8. He's a waiter.

Lesson B: I was a teacher.

Exercise 1 page 88
Before

1. was	5. was
2. was	6. were
3. were	7. was
4. was	8. was

Now

1. is	5. is
2. is	6. are
3. are	7. is
4. am	8. is

Exercise 2 page 88

1B. is	2B. is
1A. Was	2A. Was
1B. was	2B. wasn't, was

Exercise 3 page 89
1. Were they waiters before?
2. Was she a teacher before?
3. Were they electricians before?
4. Was she a manager before?
5. Was he a nurse before?

Exercise 4 page 89
1. No, he wasn't. He was a manager.
2. No, he wasn't. He was a waiter.
3. No, I wasn't. I was a nurse.
4. No, she wasn't. She was a waitress.
5. No, they weren't. They were students.

Lesson C: Can you cook?

Exercise 1 page 90
1. Yes, he can.
2. No, she can't.
3. No, they can't.
4. Yes, they can.
5. No, he can't.
6. Yes, she can.

Exercise 2 page 90
1. Vera
2. Brenda
3. Daniel
4. Mary

Exercise 3 page 91
1A. Can he cook
1B. No, he can't.
2A. Can he drive

2B. No, he can't.
3A. Can he fix a car
3B. No, he can't.
4A. Can he speak English
4B. Yes, he can.
5A. Can he work with a computer
5B. Yes, he can.

Exercise 4 page 91
1. She can paint.
2. He can take care of children.
3. They can fix cars.
4. He can drive a truck.
5. He can take care of plants.
6. She can build things.

Lesson D: Reading

Exercise 1 page 92

```
f  r  c  e  a  a  l  y  r  o
a  e  o  h  o  p  s  c  l  d
t  s  u  o  h  o  t  e  l  r
o  t  r  s  c  h  o  o  l  u
f  a  t  p  l  o  r  f  s  g
f  u  r  i  f  m  e  f  h  s
a  r  o  t  e  r  i  r  t  t
c  a  n  m  o  m  o  c  r  o
h  n  m  l  t  h  u  e  m  r
o  t  f  a  c  t  o  r  y  e
o  h  o  p  r  e  h  o  m  l
```

Exercise 2 page 92

1. hotel	6. store
2. drugstore	7. factory
3. hospital	8. office
4. home	9. school
5. restaurant	

Exercise 3 page 93
1. Hello. What's your name?
2. My name is Francisco.
3. Hi, Francisco. What job are you looking for?
4. I'm looking for a job as a salesperson.
5. OK. What can you do?
6. I can sell things. I can talk to customers.

Exercise 4 page 93
1. Yes, he is.
2. He was a salesperson in his country.
3. Now he's a busboy.
4. He wants to find a job as a salesperson.

5. He can sell things in a store. He can talk to customers.
6. Yes, he can speak several languages.

Lesson E: Writing

Exercise 1 page 94

1. Can she work with a computer?
2. Was she a nurse in her country?
3. Was he a waiter in his country?
4. Can he fix a car?
5. Is Ana looking for a job?
6. What are your skills?

Exercise 2 page 94

1A. Can	4A. Is
1B. can	4B. is
2A. Is	5A. Can
2B. was	5B. can't
3A. Can	6A. Was
3B. can't	6B. was

Exercise 3 page 94

1. work
2. restaurant
2. waiter
4. busboy
5. cook
6. manager

Exercise 4 page 95

1. Five years ago, Ana was a manager in her country.
2. Now she is a cashier.
3. She can use a cash register.
4. She can count money and talk to customers.
5. Ana and her husband are happy with their jobs in this country.
6. Before they were managers. Now they have new jobs.

Exercise 5 page 95

Jim was at Pizza Palace last Saturday. His boss was there, too. Jim was very busy. There were many customers in the restaurant. They weren't happy because their food wasn't ready. The customers were angry. They were very hungry. Jim was hungry, too. He was also tired. Jim was ready to go home!

Lesson F: Another view

Exercise 1 page 96

1. beauty salon
2. salesperson
3. give change
4. serve food
5. cars
6. fix a car
7. restaurant
8. cook
9. paint rooms
10. shopping mall

Exercise 2 page 96

Skill

1. take care of children
2. cut hair
3. clean rooms
4. work with computers
5. sell things
6. serve food

Place of work

1. day-care center
2. beauty salon
3. hotel
4. office
5. store
6. restaurant

Exercise 3 page 97

Place

1. She works in a hotel.
2. He works in a restaurant.
3. She works in a store.
4. He works in an office.
5. He works in a beauty salon.
6. He works in a day-care center.

Skill

1. She cleans rooms.
2. He serves food.
3. She sells things.
4. He works with computers.
5. He cuts hair.
6. He takes care of children.

Exercise 4 page 97

1. Yes, she is.
2. She is a certified nursing assistant.
3. No, she wasn't.
4. She works at Manor Inn Nursing Home.
5. Yes, she is.
6. She was a cashier from 2004 to 2006.

Unit 9: Daily living

Lesson A: Get ready

Exercise 1 page 98

1. iron	6. trash
2. dishes	7. vacuum
3. mop	8. wash
4. sweep	9. empty
5. clean	10. paint

Exercise 2 page 98

1. paint
2. wash
3. sweep
4. iron
5. vacuum
6. empty

Exercise 3 page 99

1. b	3. a	5. f	7. e
2. g	4. d	6. c	

Exercise 4 page 99

1. dishes	5. bills
2. floor	6. clothes
3. house	7. floor
4. rug	8. trash

Exercise 5 page 99

1. $74.99
2. Acme Vacuums
3. (514) 555-8976
4. Cincinnati
5. Ohio

Lesson B: I dusted the living room.

Exercise 1 page 100

1. cleaned	6. ironed
2. cooked	7. mopped
3. dried	8. painted
4. dusted	9. vacuumed
5. emptied	

Exercise 2 page 100

1. cleaned	6. dusted
2. painted	7. mopped
3. emptied	8. dried
4. cooked	9. vacuumed
5. ironed	

Exercise 3 page 101

1A. Did
1B. didn't, mopped
2A. Did
2B. didn't, vacuumed
3A. Did
3B. did, dried

4A. Did
4B. didn't, cleaned
5A. Did
5B. didn't, emptied
6A. Did
6B. didn't, washed
7A. Did
7B. didn't, dusted
8A. Did
8B. didn't, cleaned

Lesson C: I paid the bills.
Exercise 1 page 102

1. got
2. did
3. paid
4. made

Exercise 2 page 102

1A. got
1B. Mei did.
2A. made
2B. Jian did.
3A. did
3B. Jin did.
4A. paid
4B. Shufen did.

Exercise 3 page 103

1. cut
2. swept
3. made
4. bought

Exercise 4 page 103

1. didn't, swept
2. didn't, cut
3. did
4. didn't, made
5. didn't, bought
6. did

Lesson D: Reading
Exercise 1 page 104

o	w	k	i	t	c	h	e	n	y
s	t	o	v	e	f	o	o	d	v
s	b	l	a	u	n	d	r	y	e
p	r	v	a	c	u	u	m	m	u
o	o	g	p	a	s	s	u	m	g
n	o	n	y	e	v	t	k	o	b
g	m	a	i	l	d	p	i	w	a
e	n	g	a	r	b	a	g	e	t
m	i	r	o	n	i	n	g	r	w
z	c	d	e	f	n	q	i	o	s

Exercise 2 page 104

1. swept, broom
2. made, stove
3. cut, mower
4. washed, sponge
5. cleaned, vacuum
6. got, mail

Exercise 3 page 105

People (underlined)
Cabrera family
Mom
Dad
Yolanda
Roberto
Sara

Chores (circled)
cleaned their house
swept the kitchen
mopped the kitchen floor
cut the grass
washed the dishes
vacuumed the rugs
made the beds
emptied the trash
got the mail

Exercise 4 page 105

1. Dad
2. Sara
3. Sara
4. Roberto, Sara
5. Dad
6. Mom
7. Dad, Yolanda
8. Roberto

Exercise 5 page 105

1. No, they didn't. They cleaned it on Saturday.
2. Dad cut the grass.
3. Sara and Roberto made the beds.
4. Mom swept the kitchen.
5. No, she didn't. Yolanda washed the dishes.

Lesson E: Writing
Exercise 1 page 106

1. Jason did.
2. No, she didn't.
3. Jordan made the beds.
4. Yes, she did.
5. Linda vacuumed the rug.
6. No, he didn't.
7. No, he didn't.
8. No, he didn't.

Exercise 2 page 107

1. weekend
2. chores
3. groceries
4. grass
5. bathroom
6. floor
7. mail
8. bills
9. trash
10. laundry
11. rug
12. works

Exercise 3 page 107

Last weekend, the Johnson family did chores. Lucille bought groceries. Vince cut the grass. Lynn cleaned the bathroom and swept the floor. Nicky got the mail and paid the bills. Ida emptied the trash. Raymond did the laundry and vacuumed the rug. Everyone worked very hard.

Lesson F: Another view
Exercise 1 page 108

1. b   3. c   5. b
2. b   4. a   6. d

Exercise 2 page 109

Down
1. dusted
3. bought
4. made
5. ironed
7. emptied
9. cut

Across
2. swept
6. vacuumed
8. got
10. painted
11. paid

Unit 10: Leisure

Lesson A: Get ready
Exercise 1 page 110

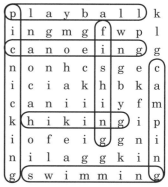

138   Answer key

Exercise 2 page 110

1. hiking
2. swimming
3. fishing
4. canoeing
5. camping
6. picnicking
7. play ball

Exercise 3 page 111

1. b   3. d   5. d
2. a   4. b   6. d

Lesson B: What did you do yesterday?

Exercise 1 page 112

1. did
2. drove
3. ate
4. went
5. had
6. made
7. read
8. saw
9. slept
10. wrote

Exercise 2 page 112

1A. go   5A. drive
1B. went   5B. drove
2A. eat   6A. read
2B. ate   6B. read
3A. do   7A. sleep
3B. went   8A. see
4A. write   8B. saw

Exercise 3 page 113

1. went hiking
2. went picnicking
3. went swimming
4. read books
5. slept late
6. went fishing
7. drank hot chocolate

Exercise 4 page 113

1. What did they do last week?
2. What did they do on Saturday?
3. What did they do on Sunday?
4. They went swimming.
5. What did they do on Tuesday?
6. They slept late.
7. What did they do on Thursday?
8. They drank hot chocolate.

Lesson C: What are you going to do?

Exercise 1 page 114

1. They are going to go to a party.
2. They are going to play soccer.
3. They are going to watch a movie.
4. She is going to drive to a lake.
5. They are going to play basketball.
6. They are going to buy clothes.

Exercise 2 page 115

1. 's going to go
2. 's going to go
3. 're going to play
4. 're going to take
5. 'm going to clean
6. 's going to buy

Exercise 3 page 115

1. going to go swimming
2. going to go shopping
3. going to cook dinner
4. going to take a vacation
5. going to rest

Lesson D: Reading

Exercise 1 page 116

1. camping
2. hiking
3. swimming
4. fishing
5. skiing
6. ice hockey
7. baseball
8. basketball
9. soccer
10. football

Exercise 2 page 116

1. was
2. drove
3. took
4. watched
5. ate
6. did
7. was
8. took
9. watched
10. went
11. ate

Exercise 3 page 117

1. He went camping with friends.
2. They went fishing.
3. They ate fish for lunch.
4. They went hiking.
5. They went swimming in the lake.
6. They went to bed late.

Exercise 4 page 117

6   2   5   3   4   1

Lesson E: Writing

Exercise 1 page 118

1. What are you going to do this weekend?
2. I'm going to go to a birthday party.
3. Who is the party for?
4. It's my sister's birthday.
5. That sounds like fun.
6. Yes, I'm going to have a lot of fun.

Exercise 2 page 118

1. What did you do last weekend?
2. We went hiking in the mountains.
3. Did you go with your son?
4. No, I went with a friend.
5. Did you go swimming?
6. Yes, we went swimming and canoeing.
7. What are you going to do next weekend?

Exercise 3 page 119

Ali had a good weekend. On Saturday, he went to a baseball game with his friend. They ate hot dogs and drank sodas. They came home at 5:00. On Sunday, Ali played soccer with his friends at the park near his house. They played all afternoon. They had a good time.

Exercise 4 page 119

1. I went to the park last weekend.
2. Maria drove to the shopping mall yesterday.
3. Ali and Miriam ate Chinese food last weekend.
4. John played soccer last weekend.
5. What are you going to do next Friday?
6. Is he going to go to the concert on Sunday?
7. He is going to ride the bus to the concert next Sunday.

Exercise 5 page 119

Susanna and Maria are going to go camping on Saturday. They need some food. They are going to buy some bread, milk, and eggs. Then they are going to drive to the beach. In the afternoon, they are going to go hiking. On Sunday morning, they are going to go swimming and fishing. They like to exercise.

Lesson F: Another view

Exercise 1 page 120

1. a	3. b	5. d
2. d	4. d	6. c

Exercise 2 page 121

Simple past

last month	last year
last night	one week ago
last Saturday	two weeks ago
last week	yesterday
last weekend	

Future

in one month	next weekend
in two days	tomorrow
in two weeks	tonight
next week	

Exercise 3 page 121

1. played	6. play
2. play	7. went
3. went	8. go
4. went	9. went
5. go	10. going to go

Illustration credits

Laurie Conley: 16, 25, 30, 41, 79, 92, 101, 106, 119

Chuck Gonzales: 39, 90, 95, 98, 69, 91, 95, 98, 107, 112

Larry Jost: 22

Frank Montagna: 26 (*bottom*), 44, 45, 62, 77, 87, 112

Monika Roe: 17, 83, 102, 103, 110

Steve Schulman: 5, 26 (*top*), 27, 31, 36

Mark Watkinson: 52, 61, 111

Phil Williams: 14, 18, 54, 58, 78, 100

Photography credits

2 ©Punchstock

4 (*clockwise from top left*) ©Mike Watson Images/ Alamy; ©Jupiter Images; ©Punchstock; ©Jupiter Images

5 (*clockwise from top left*) ©Jupiter Images; ©Alamy; ©Getty Images; ©Jupiter Images; ©Punchstock; ©Jupiter Images

7 (*clockwise from top left*) ©Jupiter Images; ©Getty Images; ©Jupiter Images; ©Alamy

9 ©Alamy

10 ©Jupiter Images

12 ©Alamy

15 (*clockwise from top left*) ©Punchstock; ©Punchstock; ©iStockphoto; ©Shutterstock; ©Morgue File

16 (*all*) ©George Kerrigan

42 ©Getty Images

50 ©Jupiter; ©Getty Images; ©Jupiter Images; ©Jupiter Images

51 (*top row, left to right*) ©Jupiter Images; ©Getty Images; ©Getty Images; (*middle row, left to right*) ©Getty Images; ©Jupiter Images;

©Punchstock; (*bottom row, left to right*) ©Getty Images; ©Alamy; ©Getty Images

65 (*top to bottom from TV*) ©Jupiter Images; ©Getty Images; ©Alamy; ©Jupiter Images

68 ©Jupiter Images

86 (*left, top to bottom*) ©Jupiter Images; ©Hemera; ©Jupiter Images; ©Jupiter Images; (*right, top to bottom*) ©Punchstock; ©Punchstock; ©Photos.com; ©Jupiter Images

88 ©Getty Images

94 ©Getty Images

99 ©Jupiter Images

114 (*clockwise from top left*) ©Veer; ©Punchstock; ©Jupiter Images; ©Jupiter Images; ©Jupiter Images; ©Veer

115 (*clockwise from top left*) ©Jupiter Images; ©Jupiter Images; ©Jupiter Images; ©Getty Images; ©Getty Images

117 ©Jupiter Images